CONTENTS

INTRODUCTION

What is society?

Human beings are social animals. They live their lives in social groups.
People are born into families. They go to schools, belong to churches
and join clubs. Human beings also work in groups and spend their
leisure time in groups.

Groups have their own ways of doing things. They expect people to
behave in certain ways. Within groups there are often pressures which
lead people to behave in the way the group expects. Groups may even
have rules which everyone is expected to follow.

A group of close friends is an example of a small group with no real
rules about what people should or should not do. Other groups are larger
and often have very many rules, and ways of enforcing them. The school
is an example of a larger group which can enforce its rules.

Human beings need groups right through their lives. We need groups
from the moment we are born until after we have died. As human beings
we live our lives in a social world.

Some groups are made up of a number of smaller groups. Different
names are given to these different groups. We often speak of
'organisations', 'communities' and 'nations'. These are different types of
group.

The name we give to the social world that we live in is *society*. The word 'society' is used in different ways. It can mean a particular group of people who come together for a particular reason. This is how it is used when we refer to a 'Model Railway Society' or 'The Allotment Society'. It can also be used to describe a larger group of people who share certain things in common. We might speak of 'British society' or even 'high society'.

Finally it can be used in a very general way to describe all of the different kind of social relationships that people have in their lives. We use this meaning of 'society' when we say that someone is 'a member of society'.

By using the term 'society' we recognise that people are not separate, isolated individuals. They are 'social beings' and can best be understood as members of social groups.

It still leaves us with questions about how groups come into being and why they are organised in the ways in which they are. These are questions about why society takes the form that it does.

Making a world

What would you do first if you landed on an uninhabited planet far out in space? You would probably begin to look for food and water, find shelter and some way to keep warm. Your first problem would be survival.

Figure 1·1

```
Space Voyager 0193E
Commander's Log : Day 1827 – Earth Year 2054

It is now five years since our mission began. When we left
Earth we had no idea of what lay ahead on our journey into
deepest space.

Thirty years ago our radio telescopes first picked up the
rogue planet hurtling through space, its orbit moving
nearer and nearer to Earth. The task of preparing the
evacuation fleet was completed with only months to spare
before the two planets collided. The aim of our journey was
to find a new home on a planet far away on the other side of
the galaxy.

We were nearly too late. The impact of the two planets
colliding was far greater than we could ever have imagined.
The shock waves which engulfed our fleet of star-ships
caused terrible damage. Many ships were destroyed. All
suffered in some way. Our ship was the only one which
managed to restore all systems and limp on towards the
chosen destination.

Of the ten thousand people who set out only a handful
remained. With great difficulty we made the transfer from
the slowly orbiting space-craft down to the surface of
Planet Alpha.

It was a strange journey. We can remember very little of it.
The magnetic storms through which we passed not only
destroyed the data-banks in the computer but affected our
memories as well.

We found that it was a good planet. There were no
intelligent life-forms and the climate was suitable. We
could now set about the task of rebuilding our world.
```

If you are not alone, surviving would be a matter of getting yourself and your companions organised. You would need to decide who does what, and when. You would even have to decide how to make decisions and what would happen when individuals didn't keep to them. In other words you would have to begin to build a kind of society.

In such a situation no one would begin from scratch. You would remember how things were done when you were young. You would have picked up ideas, beliefs and ways of behaving which would influence the way you set about the task of re-building your world.

Imagine, however, that the intense radiation in a cosmic storm through which you passed has wiped out every memory of life on Earth. You and your companions must remake your society from the beginning. How would you set about such a task if you had no knowledge at all of how things might be done?

Discussion

What would you do in each of the following situations?

1. A serious argument has developed between two of the settlers. In what ways might arguments be dealt with?
2. There are a number of young children in the group. They need to be cared for. Whoever takes on the job of caring for them cannot hunt for food or build the houses. Who should be given the task of caring for the young?
3. Some people in the group are skilled at making things. They spend all of their time doing this and do not help the rest in the search for food. How are these people to be provided for in a way which is fair to everyone?
4. One of your companions has been taking food that belonged to others. What should be done about it?
5. You have found a number of sites on which you can build the permanent homes. Some of the sites are better than others. How will you decide who is to have the best sites?
6. These permanent homes take much longer to build. They also need people with particular skills to build them. A group of settlers become full-time house-builders. How does this affect the rest?
7. As time passes life in the settlement develops into a regular routine. Many of the important decisions have been made and everyday life falls into a pattern. More children are born. To them the community exists as though it had always been there. How would you make sure that future generations did not forget the way the community came to be?

Although this has been an imaginary story, it reminds us that societies do not just happen, they are made by ordinary people trying to sort out everyday problems. Many of these problems are about survival and making a living.

In real life we do not have to build societies from scratch, or learn how to make societies work. Each of us is born into a society which already exists. We come to know the ways of that society and take them for granted.

CHAPTER 1

KNOWING ABOUT SOCIETY

Each one of us knows a great deal about society. We experience it every day of our lives. In a way we are all experts on society. We have a stock of everyday knowledge which we call *common sense*. This tells us many of the things that we need to know if we are to make sense of the world.

Common sense cannot tell us everything we need to know. What happens when we have no previous knowledge to fall back on, when we experience something for the first time, or when our common-sense knowledge lets us down?

In everyday life we take many things for granted and seldom stop to think about them. We accept things as being facts without ever stopping to ask 'how do we know?'. This is where we can use the social sciences to examine social life more deeply.

Social scientists use *evidence*, make explanations and develop theories about social life. They may observe everyday happenings. By measuring how often things happen statistics may be collected. These help us to make comparisons and to answer questions like 'how much?' or 'how often?'. There may even be experiments which explore what will happen in very special circumstances.

But, like all other knowledge, the evidence collected by social scientists also needs to be interpreted if it is to mean anything. Like everyone else, social scientists use their common knowledge of society to help them make sense of things.

Imagine you are an alien from outer space knowing nothing of earth customs. How would you explain the events shown in these photographs?

1.1   The social sciences

Social science is not just one subject. It is a collection of subjects, each concerned with a different area of life and with its own methods of study.

Economics

Economists are concerned with how people make choices. They are interested in money and how it is used, how people make decisions about spending their money, how goods are produced and how this affects the national economy. Economists use statistics to help them explain how the economy works.

Psychology

Psychologists study the behaviour of both people and animals. They try to understand many different forms of behaviour. Psychologists ask questions about how children learn, why people aren't happy in their jobs, why shoppers buy a particular brand of soap and so on. Experiments are often used by psychologists to examine behaviour.

Sociology

Sociologists are interested in social groups, such as the family, work groups, communities, clubs and religious groups. They study the ways the groups fit together into communities and into societies. Many different methods are used but surveys and observations are particularly important.

Political science

As its name suggests, political science is concerned with government and the use of power in society. Political scientists use surveys and statistics to build up a picture of the way decisions are made and who has power.

Social anthropology

While many sociologists study the lives of people in very large groups, often counted in thousands or even millions, social anthropologists study how people live in very small groups. They study societies that have not been affected by industrialisation as well as small groups within industrial societies.

Questions

1. Which of the social sciences would be most likely to tell you about the following?
   a The Bank of England   **d** Learning to talk
   b Families   **e** Income tax
   c Members of Parliament   **f** Life in a village

2. Which social sciences would use each of the following sources of information?
   a Statistics of consumer spending
   b A survey of people at work
   c An experiment into how children learn mathematics
   d A survey into people's views of government policy
   e A study of a gypsy community

1.2   Documents and experiments

Using documents

Documents are an important source of information for social scientists. They are sometimes known as 'secondary sources'. Some documents, such as letters or ancient charters, have been handed down from a long time in the past. These historical documents tell us a great deal about social life as it used to be. We can learn about life in the present from official reports and statistics as well as from newspapers and books. The main documentary sources used by social scientists are:

> The Annual Abstract of Statistics
> Economic Trends
> Social Trends
> Regional Trends
> Crime Statistics
> The General Household Survey
> Statistics of Education
> The Census

These are produced by the government. There are also many reports produced by businesses, voluntary organisations and other bodies. You will find many of these in your local library.

Experiments

Experiments are a way of studying behaviour. An experimenter starts by making a guess about why certain events take place. This guess is called an hypothesis. Anything that might influence the event being studied is called 'a variable'. In the experiment the important variables are closely controlled. Psychologists use experiments to study behaviour. A certain type of behaviour will be measured at the beginning of the experiment and at the end to discover how it has changed. Experiments often use a 'control group' which is identical to the experimental group except for the one influence, or variable, that is being studied.

CASE STUDY

Does violence on television affect children?

Some psychologists carried out an experiment into the effect that violence on television had on very young children.

A group of nursery school children were divided into four similar groups. The children in three of the groups were shown a short television film involving violence against a toy doll. The children in the fourth group watched a film in which there was no violence. Each child watched the film on their own and was then taken to another room in which there were toys similar to those which they had seen on the films.

The researchers then left each child alone for twenty minutes, whilst secretly watching them through a one-way mirror. Each action was noted. The number of violent actions was counted. The children in the first three groups played more violently than did the children from the fourth group. The researchers came to the conclusion that young children can be influenced by violence on television.

Questions
1. In which government publications would you look up:
    a the number of crimes in any one year?
    b how many teachers there are in schools in Britain?
    c how households spend their money?
    d unemployment in the regions?
2. What do we call the guess that a researcher makes?
3. In what way is the control group treated differently from the experimental group?
4. How many groups of children were studied in the experiments on the effects of television?
5. What did the control group watch?
6. What did the experimenters do when the children were taken to the room with the toys in it?
7. What did the experiment claim to prove?
8. Give two reasons why you might not agree with the experimenters' conclusion.

1.3   Surveys and observation

Surveys

Surveys are an important source of evidence for the social scientist. They involve asking people questions on a particular topic. Surveys follow a set of rules which make sure that the answers are accurate and not biased in any way.

The list of questions, known as a questionnaire must be tested through a *pilot survey*. The people to be interviewed must be chosen carefully

to represent a fair cross-section of the group or population that is being studied. This sample is probably chosen at random from a list known as a sampling frame. The sample must be large enough to allow a fair spread of views. The interviewer must behave in exactly the same way on every interview. Replies must be carefully analysed to give a final result. The replies of different groups are compared to see if there is a pattern in the answers.

CASE STUDY

What do housewives think of housework?

Ann Oakley carried out a study of housewives in North London to discover what they felt about housework. Forty names were sampled from the lists of two doctors. The women were interviewed in their homes. A questionnaire was used to make sure that each woman was asked the same questions.

Oakley found that most of the women found housework boring and monotonous. Although they worked longer hours than most factory workers they enjoyed the independence working at home gave them. Although they didn't all like housework they liked being housewives. Oakley compared the replies from women who came from different social classes.

Figure 1.2 Planning a survey

What is the subject for your survey?

What is the population you are going to study?

Will you need to take a sample from your population?

How will you collect information?
a interviews?
b questionnaires?
c observation?

What questions will you want to ask?

How are you going to analyse the results?

How will you present your findings?

Table 1.1 Answers to the question 'Do you like housework?'

Social class	Like %	Don't mind %	Dislike %	Total %
Working class	60	10	30	100
Middle class	20	10	70	100

(Source: *Sociology of Housework* by A. Oakley, Martin Robertson, 1974, Table 4.2)

Observation

We can learn a lot about social life by just watching it. Studies which use observation are said to use *ethnographic* methods. Whereas other methods intrude into people's lives the ethnographer's aim is not to intrude. Observers may sometimes join the groups they are observing. They are then participant observers. An important rule in ethnography is to cause as little disturbance to the normal pattern of events as possible.

Ethnographic studies produce different kinds of evidence from surveys and experiments. They are less likely to include pages of statistics and more likely to read like a story. The researcher tries to give an account which presents as true a picture as possible.

A Glasgow gang

Studying a teenage gang can be very difficult. If the gang know that they are being studied they may change their behaviour. James Patrick studied a gang secretly. As a young teacher in an approved school he had plenty of opportunity to get to know boys who belonged to street gangs. One of the boys, Tim, introduced him to his mates as a friend from the school.

Once he had joined the gang he had to dress and to act the part although he was very careful not to become involved in the gang's law-breaking. He kept a diary of his weekends with the gang. When he was with the gang he went to their homes, spent time hanging around street corners, and went drinking in pubs. Once he was even arrested by the police. After three months he decided that he could not carry on for any longer and the study ended. The account of his time with the gang gives an insider's view of gang life.

Questions
1. How is a questionnaire tested out?
2. What name is given to the list from which the sample is chosen?
3. Why must a sample be fairly large?
4. How did Ann Oakley carry out her study?
5. Which group of women disliked housework most?
6. Why did James Patrick study the gang in secret?
7. Is it right to study people without their permission? Why?

1.4   A survey on choices

We can understand how social scientists work if we look at the way in which we might conduct a survey in school. This survey is based on one which was originally carried out by the National Foundation for Educational Research.

The original survey studied the attitudes of young people at secondary schools who have chosen the subjects that they want to study. The survey aimed to measure how satisfied they are with the subjects they have chosen.

Figure 1.3

Subject choice opinion survey					
This is a survey on choosing subjects in school. Do you agree or disagree with the following statements? (Mark a ring around one number on each line.)					
	Agree strongly	Agree	Neither agree nor disagree	Disagree	Disagree strongly
1. I seem to be getting on well with the subjects I have chosen	5	4	3	2	1
2. Most of the subjects I chose turned out to be a bit boring	1	2	3	4	5

The researchers had to solve two problems. Firstly, how could they measure people's attitudes? Secondly, how could they be sure that they based their survey on a representative group of people?

They solved the first problem by using a questionnaire which tried to discover how satisfied the young people were on a number of statements. When all of the scores were added up it gave a number which indicated each person's level of satisfaction.

Sampling

The second problem was solved by sampling.

The whole group which is being studied is called *a population*. Sometimes the population is too large for such a survey to be done easily. You may need to use a sample. You can get as accurate a result by asking a smaller group of people who have been carefully chosen. This smaller group is called *a sample*. If your population is every student in the fourth and fifth years of the school your sample could be based on one in every ten students.

To make a sample you need a *sampling frame*. Any list which matches the population will do. Class lists or registers make good sampling frames for school surveys.

Samples can be made by taking names at random from the sampling frame. Sometimes random sampling does not give a sample which reflects the important characteristics of the whole population. There may be too many boys or not enough from certain classes.

Researchers get over this problem by using *quota samples* in which a certain number of each group are selected. The individuals are still chosen at random but only a certain quota of people with each characteristic are used.

When a very large population is being studied the researchers may use *multi-stage sampling*. A number of towns might be chosen at random. In each town two or three schools will be sampled. In each school four classes might be chosen and in each class ten pupils.

Project

1. Use the statements on 'What I think of school' to design an attitude survey with your class. Draw a bar-graph (histogram) to show your results.

Figure 1.4 What I think of school

---

1. I seem to be getting on well with the subjects I have chosen.

2. Most of the subjects I chose turned out to be a bit boring.

3. I think the subjects I have chosen will help me later on.

4. I thought I would like some of the subjects I have chosen, but I don't.

5. Even if I had the chance to change now I would still keep to the subjects I have chosen.

6. I didn't know what I was letting myself in for with some of the subjects I chose.

7. If I could choose again I would choose different subjects.

8. I'm glad I chose the subjects I did.

9. I can't really do the work in the subjects I have chosen.

10. I was lucky I was able to take all of the subjects I wanted to.

(Source: adapted from *A Matter of Choice* by Margaret Reid, Bernard Barnett and Helen Rosenberg, NFER 1974)

2. Conduct a survey of attitudes in other classes in the school. You will need to make a sample. Compare the results with those of the survey of your class. Draw graphs to show your results.

1.5   Vocabulary

Anthropology	A social science which studies the behaviour and way of life of small groups and communities through ethnographic methods.
Behaviour	Any actions made by people or animals. Behaviour may be as important as running a marathon or as ordinary as blinking.
Control group	The control group in an experiment are treated normally as a check on the effects on the experimental group.
Experimental group	The group which is being tested in an experiment.
Ethnography	A research method which is based on close observation of a group being studied and which does not intrude upon the ordinary life of the group.
Hypothesis	A statement which tries to explain a series of events and which can be proved or disproved through some form of research.
Participant observation	An ethnographic method by which the observer joins, or participates in, the group being studied.
Pilot survey	A small survey that is carried out at the beginning of a piece of research in order to test out the questionnaire and methods of study.
Population	(i) All of the people in a particular country, town or region. (ii) The whole group that is being studied in a survey or experiment.
Random sample	A selection of people from the population being studied, which is made in such a way that everyone has an equal chance of being chosen.
Sampling frame	A list that covers, or resembles, the population being studied and is used as a basis for the sampling.
Social science	A group of subjects which study social, economic and political behaviour.
Survey	A method of research involving questions and interviews.

CHAPTER 2

POPULATION

In 1801 there were 8 892 536 people in England and Wales. This did not include those in the army, nor those on board ships. One hundred years later in 1901 the population had risen to over 32 million. This time everyone was included. By 1981 there were 49 011 417 people in England and Wales on the night the Census was taken.

The population of Britain has been growing steadily for over three hundred years. The 'population explosion' began early in the nineteenth century when standards of living began to improve. By building sewers and providing supplies of clean water, local councils removed the causes of the typhoid and cholera epidemics that had killed so many people in the past. Food supplies improved and the introduction of national

Figure 2·1 Population of England and Wales 1801–1981

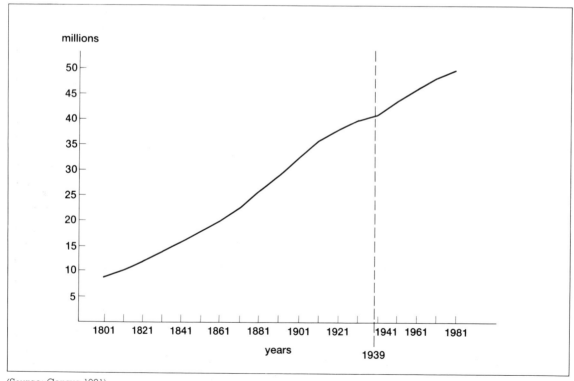

(Source: Census 1981)

insurance schemes in the early years of this century meant that even those who were unemployed did not go hungry.

As the population has grown it has changed in other ways too. People are living longer and there are more old people than there were in the past. There is movement from place to place around the country. More people are choosing to live in the southern counties of England and away from the city centres.

The population of a country does not only change when more people are born and as others die. Some leave the country and new groups of people arrive.

2.1 The Census

The government collects statistics in many ways. Births and deaths have to be registered, cars and guns have to be licensed. Industries, local councils, schools, hospitals, the police, law courts and many other bodies regularly send information to government departments. These give a picture of every aspect of life in Britain.

Every ten years a special survey is taken of the whole British population. This survey is known as the *Census*.

The first Census was taken in 1801. There has been a Census every ten years since then, except for 1941 when the nation was at war.

Figure 2.2 A page of Census data for an enumeration district.

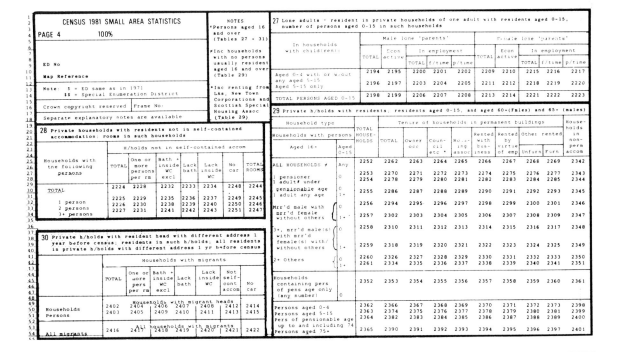

The Census is an important source of information. It is a complete survey covering every household in the country. It makes it possible to compare different districts and regions. Comparisons may also be made with previous Censuses to see how things have changed.

At one time, before computers were used, it took many years to sort out all of the information that was collected. In a modern Census, information can be published in a matter of months. When the results are available they are used by the government, by local councils and by businesses to plan for the future.

For the Census the country is divided into small areas of 150 houses. These are the enumeration districts or EDs. There are over 100 000 EDs. Census day is usually a Sunday in April. It is chosen because it is a time of the year when most people are likely to be at home. Every householder must answer a long list of questions on the Census form. This includes a list of all the people who were in the house on the night before. Hotels, hospitals, prisons and boarding houses must do the same. One in every ten householders must answer questions on a longer form. This is known as the *ten per cent sample*.

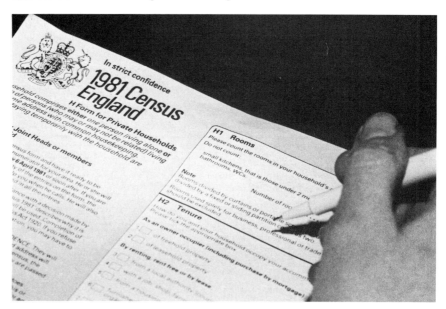

As well as counting all of the people in the country the Census form also asks questions about where they were born, what they do for a living, what sort of houses they live in and whether they own household goods like refrigerators. When all of this information has been sorted out, it is possible to get a very accurate picture of how people live in every part of the country.

One group of Census questions asks people about their homes. By comparing the answers we can get a clear picture of different living standards in different parts of the country.

Figure 2·3 Regional differences, 1981 census

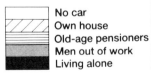

No car
Own house
Old-age pensioners
Men out of work
Living alone

(Source: Census 1981)

Questions
1. How often is the 'Census of Population' taken?
2. What is the smallest area covered by the Census called?
3. Whom must a householder include on the Census form?
4. Which area in Figure 2.3 has:
    a the largest percentage of homes rented from the local council?
    b the smallest percentage of homes without their own bathroom?
    c the largest percentage of self-contained homes?

2.2   Births and deaths

Changes in the numbers of births and deaths are an important cause
of changes in the total population. Knowing the total number of births
and deaths is not, however, as useful as knowing the birth and death
rates.

Figure 2·4 Population changes

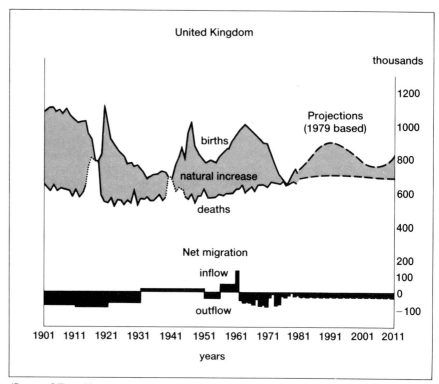

(Source: Office of Population Censuses and Surveys)

Birth rates

The *birth rate* compares the number of births to the total size of the
population. It is measured by the number of births per thousand of the
total population each year. The *death rate*, on the other hand, is the
number of deaths per thousand of the total population each year. These
rates tell us the speed at which changes are taking place in just the
same way that miles or kilometres-per-hour tell us the rate at which
a car is moving.

Birth rates

The birth rate is influenced by the number of couples who are having children. This is also influenced by the number of women who are at the age when they are able to have children. This is measured by the *fertility rate*. Until the end of the 1960s birth rates in Britain were rising but in the early 1970s the birth rate began to fall.

This happened when couples began to wait a little longer before they started a family. Some decided to have fewer children, or to have no children at all. Smaller families became more fashionable. More women wanted to have a career of their own before having children. Contraception made it possible for couples to plan their families in this way.

When there is a fall in the birth rate the effects are felt for many years. Fewer places are needed in nursery schools. If there are less children there is less demand for prams, baby clothes and toys. Primary and secondary schools will need fewer teachers. Schools will be closed. There will be fewer people at college and university, and eventually fewer workers for industry. Fewer children born now means fewer parents in twenty years time.

Figure 2·5 Birth rates

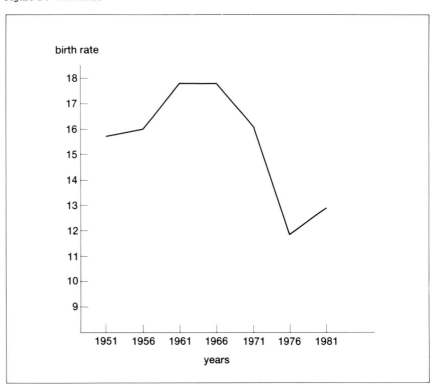

(Source: *Social Trends*, 1984, Table 1·8)

Figure 2·6 Fertility rates

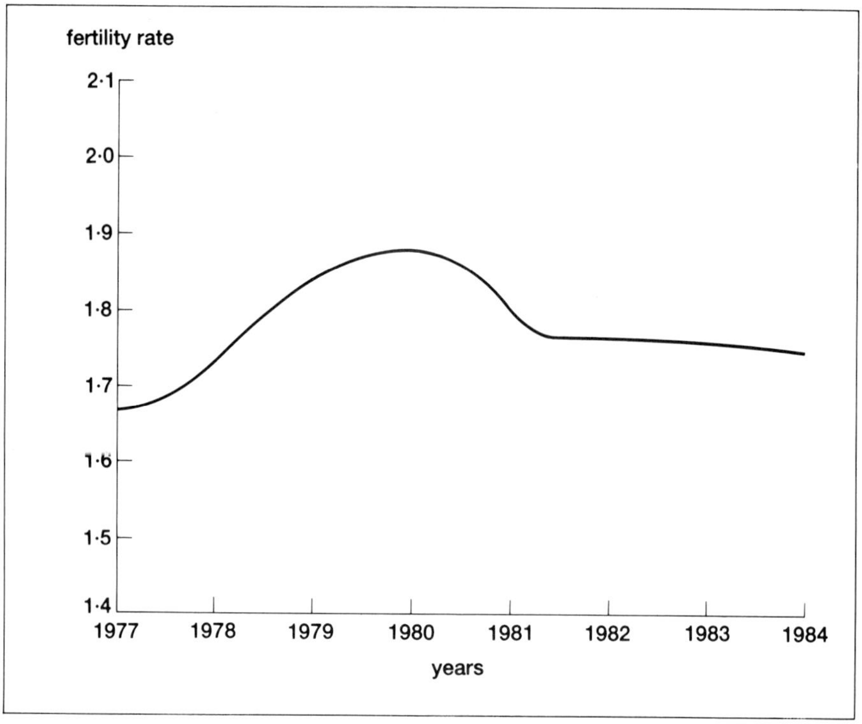

(Source: *OPCS Monitor*)

Death rates

Death rates do not change in quite the same way as birth rates. Apart from some ups-and-downs from year to year there have been no great changes in the death rate for over 50 years. Looked at more closely, certain patterns can be seen. People are living longer and, on average, women live longer than men. The population as a whole is getting older. This increases demand for health and welfare services and government spending on pensions. The greatest increases have been in the number of very old people – over 85. As women live longer than men this means that there are two women to every man in the 75–84 age group and four women to every man over 85.

Death rates are highest for the very old and for the very young. The death rate for young children has fallen steadily over the past thirty years. The infant mortality rate measures the number of deaths of children under one year of age, per thousand live births per year.

Although fewer babies die now than would have died in the past, the chances of babies surviving the first year still depend upon the circumstances into which they are born.

Table 2.1   Infant mortality

	Legitimate births	Illegitimate births
1970/2	17.7	—
1976	13.3	21.1
1978	12.4	18.2
1979	11.8	19.1
1980	11.2	16.7
1981	10.2	15.2

(Source: *Social Trends*, 1985, Table 7.2, HMSO)

Figure 2·7 Infant mortality (per 1000 and social class)

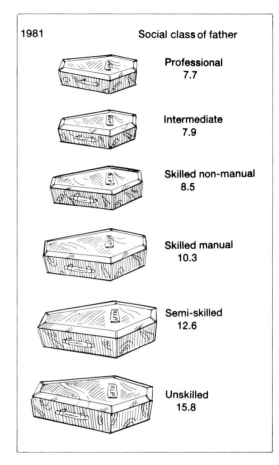

1981 — Social class of father

Professional 7.7

Intermediate 7.9

Skilled non-manual 8.5

Skilled manual 10.3

Semi-skilled 12.6

Unskilled 15.8

(Source: *Social Trends*, 1985, Table 7·2, HMSO)

Questions

1. What do you understand by the following?
   a Birth rate
   b Death rate
   c Fertility rate
   d Infant mortality rate
2. What might be the effects of a fall in the birth rate on:
   a infant schools?
   b baby-wear manufacturers?
   c hospitals?
3. What might be the effect of a fall in death rates on:
   a hospitals?
   b local welfare services?
   c house prices in 'retirement resorts' on the south coast?

2.3 Migration

The movement of people from place to place is known as *migration*.
It happens when people move from one part of a country to live
elsewhere, and when they leave one country to settle in another country.
Moving into a country is called *immigration* and the people who arrive
are immigrants. When people move out of a country it is *emigration*
and those who leave are emigrants.

Most migration takes place within a country. In Britain there is a steady
movement of people from the north towards the south. There is also
a movement of people out of the city centres into the suburbs and out
to the countryside.

Figure 2·8 Where will you be in AD2000? Estimated population growth by 2001

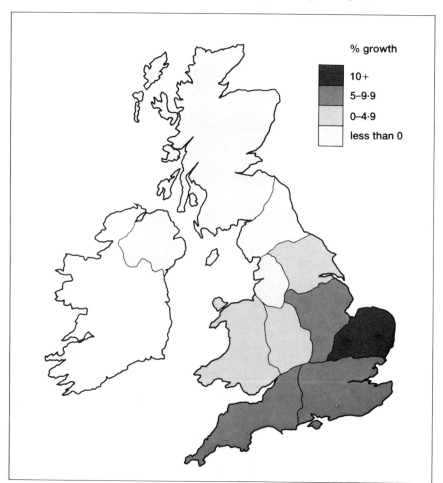

(Source: *The Facts of Everyday Life* by T. Osman, Faber and Faber, 1985, Table 85)

It is a very big decision for a family to leave its home and seek a new life elsewhere. It is not a decision that is taken without careful thought. The migrant faces both a push and a pull. The 'push' comes from the poor conditions in the home country. The 'pull' is provided by the thought of a better life elsewhere. For some people there is no choice. They may be refugees, forced to move.

Migration usually follows a pattern. One or two members of a family or a village will be the first to emigrate. They may be helped by fellow countrymen who are already settled in the new country. They will find a job and start saving money. In time they may be able to buy a house. Only then, often after many years, will they send for the rest of the family. Some migrants may never settle permanently in the new country. They may work to earn the money to send back to their family far away on the other side of the world. Only when they retire will they go back to live in their home village or town. Some communities depend upon the remittances that are sent by their migrant workers.

Britain has always been a nation of migrants. The Romans came and built their roads and a wall to keep out the tribesmen to the north. There were Saxons and later Vikings who farmed the land and traded with the other inhabitants. William the Conqueror came with his Norman knights. Since then there have been French protestants and Polish Jews fleeing from persecution, Irish peasant farmers forced out by the potato famine, people from the Caribbean, from India and from Pakistan seeking work, as well as people from Australia, New Zealand and South Africa and many other parts of the world.

At the same time that people have been coming to Britain, others have been looking for a new life overseas. British migrants settled in the American colonies, in Africa, Australia and in New Zealand.

Migration is a two-way process. It involves 'flows' of people into and out of the country. The difference between the number of immigrants and the number of emigrants is known as 'net migration'. In recent years Britain has become a country of net emigration. More people have left than have come into the country. This is mainly a result of Britain's very strict immigration laws.

Many thousands of Asians left Uganda. They arrived at Stansted airport to start a new life in Britain.

Figure 2·9 Net migration, 1980—82 (thousands)

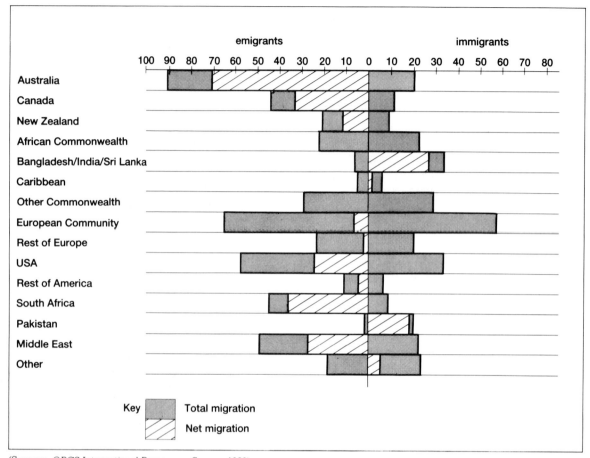

(Source: *OPCS International Passenger Survey*, 1983)

CASE STUDY

San Tin

San Tin is on the mainland of Hong Kong, not far from the Chinese border.
At one time the villagers made a living selling rice in the markets of
Hong Kong. Cheaper rice from other regions meant that the villagers
had to find other ways to live.

    The villagers had to emigrate to find work. The first migrants came
to Britain where they set up Chinese restaurants. Other villagers joined
them and soon San Tin came to rely on the money sent home by the
migrants. As well as providing jobs and a place to live, the network
of village families also helped with travel and with setting up in business.
There were close links between those who lived in Britain and their
families in Hong Kong. When they retired the migrants returned
permanently to settle once more in San Tin.

2.4   Black Britons

There have been black people in Britain since the sixteenth century. Some came to Britain to work as servants to rich noblemen. Many were slaves. By the end of the eighteenth century there were large black communities in many of the main ports like London and Liverpool.

Between 1950 and 1961 immigration from the Caribbean and from India was encouraged by British employers who needed workers for the railways, buses and hospitals. In 1972 many thousands of Asians were expelled from Uganda by President Idi Amin. Most of them came to Britain. Since 1961 the changes in immigration laws have cut the flow of black immigrants to a few thousand a year.

Figure 2·10 Ethnic origins (%)

White 95.5

Indian 1.5

Afro-Caribbean 1.0

Pakistan 0.5

Other 1.5

Black men and women have made an important contribution to athletics and many other areas of life.

Black people in Britain come from many parts of the world. As well as those from the Caribbean and East Africa, others came from India, Pakistan and Bangladesh. Most of the young people have been born in Britain.

It is very often the young people who make the move to a new country. This means that immigrants as a group are usually younger than the rest of the community. They are often at the stage in their lives when they are just starting their families. This has meant that the population of black Britons has a larger proportion of young people than the white population. One in every four of the total population is under 16 years of age compared to one in three of those who are of Caribbean or Asian origin.

The black population is not evenly spread throughout the country. London, Birmingham and Manchester have large black communities. In Leicester and Bradford there are more Asians whereas in Leeds and Bristol there are mainly people of Afro-Caribbean origin.

CASE STUDY

Donald Hinds

Donald Hinds was brought up in Jamaica. His family were used to travelling. In his village nearly every family knew someone who lived abroad. When he left school at 18 Donald travelled to London to join his mother.

He arrived in Britain in August 1955 on board the SS *Auriga* and had soon found a job with London Transport. Finding a place to live was not easy. Many white people would not let rooms to black people.

When he was not working as a bus conductor Donald was studying. He took GCE 'O' Levels and 'A' Levels and then went on to take a degree with the Open University. In 1965 he left London Transport to write a book about the experience of black people coming to live in England.

After working for the Post Office Donald Hinds decided to become a teacher. His wife Dawn, who is also from Jamaica, is a social worker. They have three daughters.

Project

Migration affects many more people than just those who left their homes in the Caribbean or in India to settle in Britain.

There are very few families that have not migrated at some time. How many of the people in your class live in the same house that their parents' were born in? Migration can involve journeys of 5 kilometres, 50 kilometres or 5000 kilometres.

Carry out a migration survey. Each person in the class needs to find out where their parents were born, and if possible, where their grandparents were born.

Mark the places that the families came from on a map of the world.

2.5   Organising the evidence

The amount of information provided by the Census and by social surveys is so vast that it is almost impossible to use unless it is broken down into smaller pieces. All evidence has to be organised in a way which makes it easier to understand.

Often this means looking for patterns in the evidence and for ways of sorting it into groups. Social scientists look for categories which fit the evidence. Some categories are used regularly in most research. For example, the Census sorts its evidence by different parts of the country. This may be by large regions, by counties, towns or even parishes. Sex and age are other categories that are regularly used.

One of the most important ways of organising evidence uses the idea

Figure 2.11 Ages of marriage

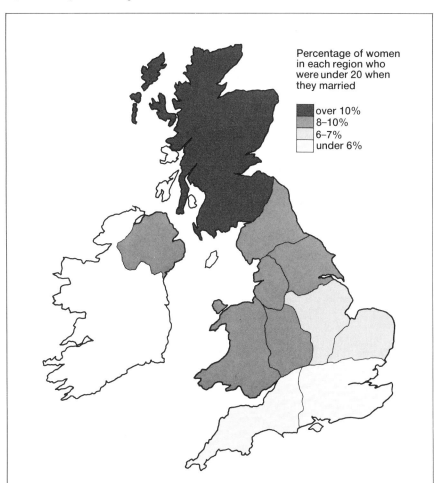

Percentage of women in each region who were under 20 when they married

over 10%
8–10%
6–7%
under 6%

(Source: *The Facts of Everyday Life* by T. Osman, Faber and Faber, 1985)

of *social class*. Like many concepts used in social science the idea of social class is also used in everyday life. Most people know what they mean by 'upper class', 'middle class' or 'working class'. They usually have some idea of which class they would put themselves into. Social

Karl Marx was born in Germany in 1818. He spent much of his life in London.

scientists try to use social class in a more exact way. Even then there are different ways in which it can be used.

Knowing someone's social class tells you something about their position in society. Social classes are often thought of as 'upper', 'middle' and 'lower'. There is some form of 'ranking'. The ranking may be very finely done with a large number of different groups, one above the other. The Hindu *caste* system has very fine rankings. People are born into castes and remain in them throughout their lives.

Class may also use a very broad ranking with only two groups, one upper and one lower. The great nineteenth-century writer Karl Marx thought that there were only two classes. He called them the bourgeoisie, or middle class, and the proletariat, or working class. In his view class depended upon the way people earned their living.

When social class is used to organise evidence from the Census or from social surveys it is based on the person's job or occupation. These are arranged in a number of groups which have been shown to share many things in common. These classes are usually known by numbers. An important dividing line is between manual work, which involves making things, and non-manual work such as office jobs and shopwork.

Social class is an important category for social scientists because different classes do have different views and behave differently. It is also something that most people recognise even if they would not always agree with the social scientists.

Instead of the six groups in the Registrar General's Classification, market research organisations sometimes use a similar system using the letters A to E. The jobs that people do can also be sorted into 17 socio-economic groups or SEGS.

Figure 2.12 The Registrar General's social classification

Class I professional	including: doctors, solicitors, university lecturers, company directors	(A)
Class II managerial and technical	including: managers, librarians, teachers, nurses, owners of small businesses etc.	(B)
Class III (non-manual) clerical and supervisory	including: clerks, salespersons, police constables, shop assistants	(C1)
Class III (manual) skilled trades	including: carpenter, cook, driver, electrician	(C2)
Class IV semi-skilled	including: bus conductor, fitter, farm worker, store-keeper	(D)
Class V unskilled	including: labourer, kitchen hand, porter, office cleaner	(E)

2.6 Vocabulary

Birth rate	The number of children born for every thousand of total population each year.
The Census	A survey of all of the people in the country which is carried out every ten years.
Death rate	The number of people who die for every thousand of total population each year.
Emigration	The movement of people out of a country.
Fertility rate	The number of births to every thousand women of child-bearing age per year.
Immigration	The movement of people into a country
Infant mortality rate	The number of children who die before they reach the age of one year for every thousand children born alive.
Migration	The movement and settlement of people from place to place within a country or between countries.
New Commonwealth	Countries which were once British colonies and from which the majority of black migrants came.
Old Commonwealth	Former British colonies which had largely white populations.
Social class	A division of social groups on the basis of people's occupations or jobs.
Socio-economic group (SEG)	A method of classification, used in official statistics, which places individuals into 17 groups according to their job or occupation.

CHAPTER 3

CULTURE AND SOCIALISATION

3.1 Culture

Every social group has its own *culture*.   Our culture includes:

the kind of homes we live in
the languages we speak
the way we dress
the food we eat

the way we earn our living
our religious beliefs
our system of politics.

These things which make up our culture did not just happen by accident. They are the result of the actions of men and women in the past. We can think of culture as something that people have made.

A newly-born baby knows nothing of the culture into which it has been born. Culture has to be learned and much of our early life is taken up with this learning. We learn and re-learn the culture of our society through socialisation.

We learn in many ways. Our families teach us a great deal. In many societies there are schools. We also learn from our friends and from

A Chinese dragon in the Soho festival is part of the culture of the Chinese community.

people we meet in many different situations.

As a baby learns to live in the world so he or she gradually becomes more of a person. Little by little a baby begins to do things for itself, to decide for itself, and to have a mind of its own.

By making their own decisions people are able to change the way they, and others, live and think. They can re-make the culture, changing it to fit new circumstances and new ideas.

3.2   Heredity and environment

The human body is made up of millions of tiny cells. They are so small that they can only be seen under microscopes. Inside each cell are the chemical instructions that enable the cell to grow in a particular way. These instructions are called chromosomes. There are 46 chromosomes, arranged in pairs inside nearly every human cell. Each chromosome carries an exact number of genes and it is these which determine the way you grow.

A baby is conceived when a sperm from the father fertilises the ovum in the mother's womb. The sperm and the ovum are different from other cells. They only contain 23 chromosomes. In coming together they combine to give the new human being its unique pattern of 46 *chromosomes*. Each individual, therefore, receives some cells from the mother and some from the father. This is the basis of heredity.

Heredity influences you in a number of ways. The colour of your hair or your eyes, for example, is a result of *heredity*. There are other things about you which are not a result of heredity. It does not influence the language you speak, for example. Those things which are not hereditary are the result of influences within our *environment*. Sometimes heredity and environment may work together to have an effect on the sort of person you are. If you are tall it may be because you have inherited 'tallness' from your parents. It may also be because you eat the right sort of food and have plenty of healthy exercise. Or it may be the result

Human sperm magnified one thousand times.   Ova developing inside the ovary before being released into the womb.

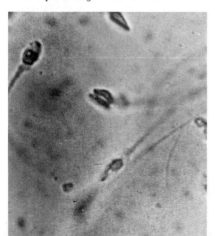
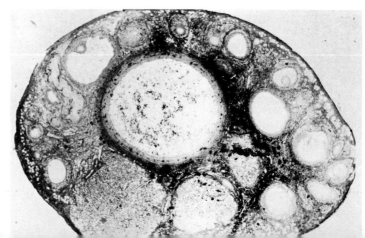

Figure 3·1 Each person receives two genes for hair colour. They have red hair when they inherit two red genes. Dark haired parents may have a red haired child

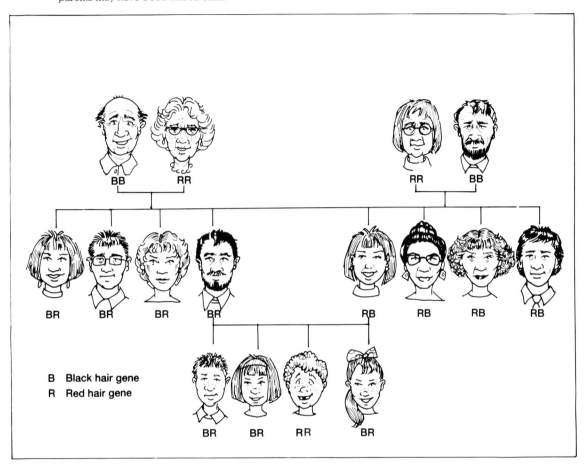

B   Black hair gene
R   Red hair gene

of a combination of inheritance and environment.

Your environment may be physical or social. The physical environment is the environment of things and objects. The house you live in, the neighbourhood and even your food are part of the physical environment. The social environment is the environment of people and includes your family, friends, and people at school or work.

Questions
1. How many chromosomes are there in each human cell?
2. Which cells have half of this number? Why?
3. How is it that parents with dark hair could have a red-haired child?
4. Give two examples of things that are part of:
   a your physical environment,
   b your social environment.

Nature and nurture

It is very difficult to know how far any one person is influenced by heredity or by their social or physical environment. If someone is a good musician, is it because they inherited musical ability from their parents, or because they grew up in a family where there was lots of music? It may be because they were given a musical instrument when they were young. Again, it could be a combination of all of these things. Psychologists describe this as the nature-nurture problem. Which is the main influence on the sort of person you are: nature (heredity) or nurture (environment)? It is a difficult question to answer.

Discussion

When psychologists try to answer the nature-nurture problem they need to find a way of keeping the effects of heredity and environment separate. There are many people who live in similar environments. There are very few people who have the same genes. In fact the only way two people can have the same genes is when they come from the same ovum fertilised by the same sperm. This only happens when identical twins are born. Look carefully at the table.

1. Where would you put the following groups on the table?
    a Two sisters who are not twins but are brought up together and go to the same schools.
    b Identical twins who are brought up in different homes.
    c Any group of total strangers.
    d Identical twins who are brought up together.

Figure 3.2 Heredity and environment

		Same heredity	Different heredity
Same environment		?	?
Different environment		?	Any group of total strangers

2. How might these different groups of people be used to try to answer the 'nature-nurture problem'?

3.3 Roles and socialisation

Birthdays are times for giving presents and having a celebration. Some birthdays are special. On your eighteenth birthday you 'come-of-age' and it can be an occasion for a special celebration.

A procession of Irish children on their way to their first communion.

There are other important points in our lives which are marked by celebrations: a baptism, bar mitzvah, first communion, a wedding, a retirement party. Each celebration marks a change of status. The baby becomes a child, the child becomes a teenager, the teenager becomes an adult.

The change from one status to another is known as *the status passage*. With each new status there are new *roles* to learn.

In all societies the change from the status of child to adult is an important event. When a girl of the MaButi people of Central Africa reaches womanhood the festivities last for days. At his Bar Mitzvah a Jewish boy becomes a man.

Within most small-scale societies each young person goes through a single change from child to adult. It takes place as soon as he or she is able to take on adult responsibilities at around 13 or 14 years of age. Industrialised societies often delay the time when children become adults. There is often a period between childhood and adulthood. We call this adolescence, or 'teenage'. At this part of your life you are no longer a child, but not quite an adult.

While we are still young we learn the very basic things that we need if we are to live in social groups. We come to know right from wrong, how to keep ourselves clean and tidy, and how to get on with other people. We also begin to develop a personality with our own likes and dislikes. This process of becoming a person is known as primary socialisation and it takes place within the family.

Everyone has certain roles in life. In a family there are roles of mother, father, son, daughter, brother and sister. Outside the family there are more roles: pupil, student, teacher, shop assistant and so on. We can recognise when someone is in a particular role in a number of ways.

Figure 3·3 Roles

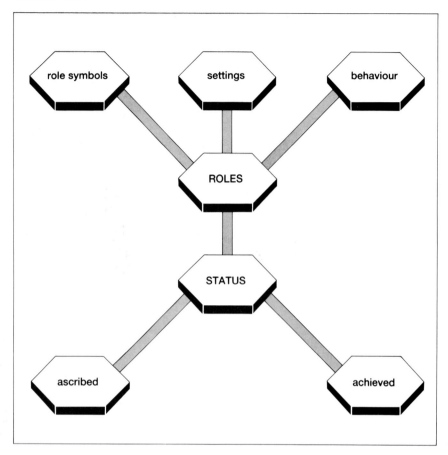

We recognise the police by their uniform, a mayor from the chain-of-office which is worn. These are role symbols. We might, however, recognise a doctor from the surroundings or setting in which we meet him or her, or from his or her behaviour. Socialisation helps us to recognise the symbols, settings and behaviour that go with particular roles.

Roles are also linked to a certain position, or status, in life. We may be born to that position, in which case the role is said to be *ascribed*, or we have to *achieve* it through our own efforts.

Social scientists have taken the idea of 'a role' from the theatre where actors perform roles that are in the script of the play. In real life roles are not quite like that. We can often change the ways in which we perform the role and make the role fit ourselves. We do not always have to fit into roles that are given to us. Although there is often very strong pressure to make us keep to certain roles we do have a choice. If this were not so we would all end up as carbon copies of other people.

This process of learning about roles which goes on right through our lives is called *secondary socialisation*.

Our socialisation is influenced by many groups within our society. These groups can be called *agents of socialisation*. The family is one of these agents of socialisation. Others would be school, the mass media, religious groups and other groups to which we might belong and which might influence our behaviour and our ideas.

Questions
1. Which form of socialisation takes place mainly within the family?
2. Write down three 'agents of socialisation' other than the family?
3. Make a list of the different roles that you perform in everyday life. Against each role write down the behaviour that is expected of you.
4. Look carefully at each photograph.
   a What is the setting?
   b What symbols are there that tell us about different roles?
   c Can you arrange the roles in any order of status?
   d What behaviour would you expect from someone in each of the roles?

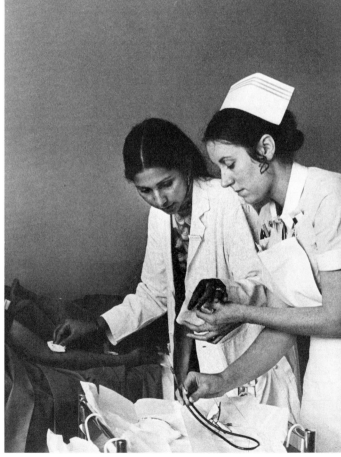

3.4   The !Kung San of the Kalahari

Figure 3·4

Kalahari
Desert

The Kalahari Desert is a vast flat area of scrubland and bush stretching across southern Africa. The !Kung live by hunting animals and by gathering nuts, berries and roots. People who live in this way are known as hunters and gatherers.

Each !Kung band is made up of thirty to forty people in a number of families. They build their camps near water or in good hunting places. Their round shelters, made of branches covered with grass or leaves, provide shade from the hot sun and a place for the family to store its belongings. The 8–10 shelters in each encampment are built in a circle facing inwards towards the fires on which the !Kung cook. In the centre of the camp there is a clearing where the children play.

Unless they are out gathering food with the women, or following the men on a hunting trip, the children will spend most of their time within the circle of shelters. They are seldom far away from adults or older children. If the children's own parents are not nearby there will be other adults in the camp who will take care of them. There are very few times when anyone is completely on their own.

Within each small band there are likely to be older and younger children but few of the same age. In their games the children do not compete. If they did the older children would always win. There are

A !Kung camp among the trees during the rainy season.

no team games with rules and groups playing against each other. Competition is not found in !Kung society. Games are played for fun and not to show that anyone is better than the rest.

Often their games involve playing at hunting, or digging for roots. Young children may make little bows of wood with arrows of grass stems to go hunting beetles and grasshoppers. They will bring back their catch to be cooked over imaginary camp-fires. At three or four years of age it is often the boys who play at hunters while the girls play at preparing and cooking the food. The older boys will hunt small birds and animals and practise tracking animals across the bushland. From the age of 12 or 13 they will begin to go out hunting with the men while the girls will join the women in gathering expeditions.

Growing-up in the camp the children learn what it means to belong to the !Kung band. They are seldom lonely. There is always someone to be near and to talk to. There are strong feelings of co-operation and sharing. Without the help of the rest of the band no individual would survive in the Kalahari.

Discussion

We can use five headings to organise what we have read about growing-up in the Kalahari:

Who takes care of young children?
Who forms the children's group?
What sort of games do they play?
How do they learn the roles of adults?
How close is the community?

Can you use the same headings to organise what you know about growing-up in Britain? Use the grid to help you.

Figure 3.5

	!Kung	Britain
Who takes care of young children?		
Who forms the children's group?	All of different ages	
What sort of games do they play?		Team games and competitions
How do they learn the roles of adults?		
How close is the community?	Very close and dependent on each other	

3.5   Childhood and adolescence

Two hundred years ago children were thought to be naturally sinful
creatures who needed to be moulded into godly ways. People believed
that if they were left to themselves children would be corrupted by the
devil. When artists painted children they painted them as small adults.
Childhood as we know it hardly existed.

At the beginning of the nineteenth century ideas began to change.
Some people thought that children were born pure but that they were
corrupted by the world. Many children were sent to work in factories
and mines for long hours every day. They often lived in slum districts
and in poor housing. People began to believe that it was the conditions
in which children lived and worked which caused them harm. These
new ideas led to laws which protected children. Factory Acts prevented
young children from being sent out to work. Education Acts began to
provide money for schools at which children could learn. Many people
felt that children would develop best if they were allowed to grow in

An advertisement in a modern clothes catalogue shows children as active and adventurous.

as natural a way as possible, away from the influence of the industrial cities. Orphans and children in trouble were often sent to homes out in the countryside where they could grow in more natural surroundings.

Children's play was now seen as part of growing up, not just a childish waste of time. It was realised that children needed toys which encouraged them to think for themselves and to use their imagination. Artists began to paint children differently. They were shown in more natural settings, often with animals. Childhood had been invented.

Although the children in this Victorian engraving are playing with children's toys they are dressed as little adults.

DESIGNED FOR

THE LADIES' GAZETTE OF FASHION

Questions
1. How have ideas about childhood changed?
2. How did the environment in the cities affect children?
3. Which laws were passed to protect children?
4. Make a collection of newspaper advertisements which include children. What do they tell us about modern ideas of childhood?

If the nineteenth century saw the invention of childhood then it was the second half of the twentieth century that invented the teenager.

Adolescence is the period between childhood and adulthood from the ages of 11 or 12 to 18 or 19. *Puberty* marks the beginning of adolescence. This is when the body of the child begins to change and take on the features of the adult. There is often a rapid increase in height.

For a girl this is the time that the breasts start to form, the hips widen and menstruation starts. For boys the voice deepens, the beard starts to grow and the testes drop. Alongside these physical changes there are also emotional changes.

In many societies puberty has marked the beginning of adult life with all the rights and responsibilities of the adult. In our society these rights and responsibilities are often delayed until long after most individuals are physically grown up. By the age of 18 most rights have been gained, some are gained much earlier and some are not gained until later. For much of this time most adolescents are dependent upon their parents for their income and their upkeep.

Adolescence is also the time of 'the teenager'. Teenage has taken its place alongside childhood and adulthood as a recognised stage in life. It has its own entertainment, fashions, youth clubs and life styles. We could even say that youth has its own culture.

Questions
1. What physical changes take place at adolescence?
2. Why are young people in Britain dependent upon their parents for so long?
3. 'Teenager' means different things to different people. Compare the way teenagers are seen in national newspapers and in magazines bought by young people.

3.6 Youth culture

So far we have seen culture as something that exists within each society and is handed on from one generation to the next. If you think back to the problems of the space travellers in Chapter 1 you will understand why that is not the only way to understand the concept of culture.

Although we may sometimes think that people in Britain share a common culture, in practice there are many different ways of life that might be called 'British'. There are regional differences, social class differences and ethnic differences. These differences do not lead to a whole variety of different cultures. Instead they create different sub-cultures within the wider 'British culture'. Sometimes these different sub-cultures overlap.

As well as difference of region, social class and race, there are also differences of age. Age is another basis for a sub-culture. This can be seen when we consider the concept of youth sub-culture.

Young people are very much part of the wider culture. They are growing up within it and are often made to conform to it. This doesn't mean that they always accept it. They are often able to change it. On the whole, the evidence suggests that on many of the important issues young people share many of the views held by older generations.

Figure 3·6 When can you . . .?

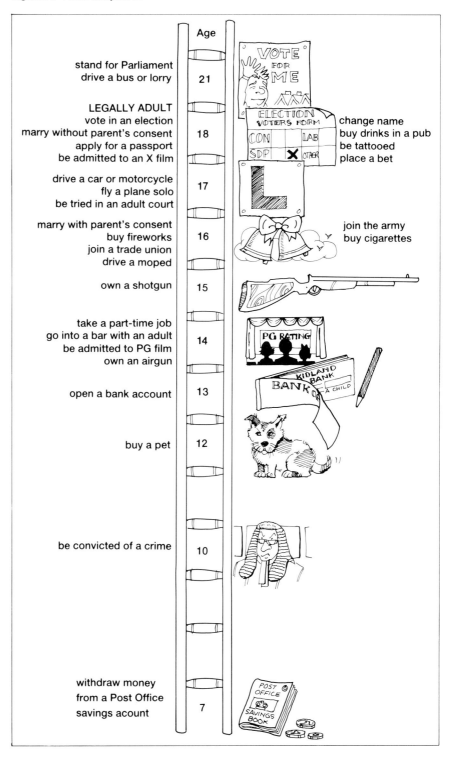

Symbols

As well as sharing in the wider culture young people are also able to make a culture of their own. This can be seen in the way they dress, the music they enjoy and in the language they speak. Youth culture may also include particular ways of behaving, which we can call rituals.

All of these things – dress, music, language and ritual – are *symbols* which are made and used by young people. Sometimes these symbols can be used as a way of resisting other groups. They can be a way of saying 'this is how I feel – keep away'. As well as keeping the youth groups apart from the older society – and from other young people – the symbols also help to keep the youth group together, giving them something to share in.

Just as it would be wrong to think that there is only one culture it would also be wrong to think that culture never changes.

Project

Imagine that you are a visitor from another planet in human form. Your mission is to prepare an ethnographic study of youth sub-culture. Your report – which can use pictures and sounds as well as words – needs to be based on the symbols of youth culture: dress, music, language and rituals.

3.7 Gender

Learning to behave in a way suited to our sex is an important part of our socialisation. Whether we are male or female depends upon the particular pattern of chromosomes inherited from our parents. It is part of our biology.

How men and women organise their lives need not be influenced by our biology. Whether women stay at home to look after children or go out and drive bulldozers is a social matter and not a biological one. We would say that such things are a matter of *gender*. Each society has its own ideas about the roles which go with each gender. This is part of culture. This means that we gain our sense of gender through socialisation. It is something that is learned.

The idea that some people learn to be boys and men while others learn to be girls and women may seem rather strange. After all we usually think that being masculine or feminine is natural. It is thought to be something that we are born with. Apart from the shapes of our bodies and our ability to have babies there are very few real differences between men and women. Women are in many ways physically stronger than men. They live longer and are less likely to suffer from certain diseases. Men can generally run faster and lift heavier weights. On the other hand the best women athletes can run faster, throw further and lift more than can most men. Many of the differences that we take to be 'natural' are in fact social.

Discussion

Which of the following are examples of sex differences and which are differences of gender?
1. Most top managers in industry are men.
2. Women are more likely than men to become nurses and typists.
3. Women generally have wider hips and narrower waists than men.
4. Men are better at jobs like lorry-driving and coal-mining.
5. It is a woman's job to stay at home and look after the children.
6. Boys are better at science subjects whereas girls do better at languages.
7. On average men are slightly taller than women.
8. Women wear brighter clothes than most men.

Project: gender and comics

The mass media is an agent of socialisation. Children learn about social roles and gender from television, magazines and comics.

Comics are aimed at different groups of children. There are comics which cater for younger children and those that are for teenagers. There are also comics for boys and comics for girls. The aim of this project is to investigate the hypothesis that gender influences the way roles are presented in comics. Do children's comics present men and women differently? If they do, does it affect how children might learn about their roles in adult life?

Make a collection of children's comics making sure that you have some that are intended for boys and some intended for girls. Each comic will probably include some stories, feature articles and advertisements. Look carefully at the stories. Make a summary of each story using the chart below.

Figure 3.9

Research project: children's comics and views of gender					
Title of comic					
Target audience	Boys/girls	Under 7	7–12	13–16	16+
Story title					
Brief description of the main characters					
Outline of the story including: locations, plot, outcome					

Figure 3·7

(Sources: *Judy and Tracy*, 4 May 1985, DC Thomson; *Champ*, 4 May 1985, DC Thomson)

Discussion

1. How does each story present:
   a male roles   **b** female roles?
2. Does each story present men and women in real-life situations?
3. Is each story likely to teach young people what it means to be either feminine or masculine?

Compare your answers for boys' and girls' comics. What differences are there? Do they present different views of the world and different gender roles?

You will probably find that boys' comics tend to use many different settings. They could be anywhere in the universe. There is also more action. Girls' stories take place in places that are more familiar, around home, at school and so on. They are more likely to be about relationships with other people.

3.8 Vocabulary

Achieved role	A position in society which has been gained through your own efforts and not handed down at birth.
Adolescence	The stage of your life between childhood and adulthood, sometimes known as 'teenage'.
Agent of socialisation	Any social group, organisation or other body which in some way helps to socialise individuals.
Ascribed role	A position in society which is handed down at birth.
Chromosome	A tiny thread-like structure in each living cell which carries the genes.
Culture	The customs, beliefs and man-made objects of a particular group of people.
Environment	Those influences which are outside of the individual. They may be either social or physical.
Genes	The parts of cells in living bodies which control heredity.
Hunters and gatherers	Simple communities which make their living by hunting animals and by gathering roots and berries.
Ritual	The behaviour which is used by people who belong to a group which is generally seen to be typical of that group.
Role	The behaviour that is expected from someone who occupies a particular social position.
Socialisation	The process of learning norms and roles.
Status	The social position held by someone.
Status passage	The ceremony which marks the movement from one status to another.
Symbol	Anything which in some way communicates a message. Symbols can include words, appearance, signs, gestures and actions.

CHAPTER 4

MARRIAGE AND THE FAMILY

All societies must find a way to deal with the problem of producing and rearing children.

That does not mean that all societies come to the same solution. What is meant by 'marriage' or by 'family' can be very different in different areas of the world. Ideas of marriage and the family are changing in our own society.

Marriage and families are not only about bringing-up children. They are also about people sharing their lives. Marriage and the family are also important in handing-on the possessions and property of one generation to the next generation.

At the very simplest level, inheritance is the way we pass on our names. It is also the way in which wealth or even positions of power and status can be passed on.

Inheritance is thought to be so important that in all communities there are laws and rules which govern it. People write wills which lay down how their possessions will be handed on.

4.1 Marriage

Marriage can mean different things. There are different ways of becoming married, different ways of choosing a partner, and differences in the legal form that marriage can take.

In Britain, marriage usually involves one man marrying one woman. We would say that marriage is *monogamous*. There are laws which make marriages of more than two people illegal. This crime is called *bigamy*. In other parts of the world it is acceptable for some people to have more than one partner. This is called *polygamy* and may involve one man with a number of wives (*polygyny*), or one woman with more than one husband (*polyandry*).

Finding a partner is often thought to be a matter of chance. The romantic stories tell you that 'one day Mr Right will come along', or you will meet the 'girl of your dreams'. Real life courtship is rather different.

For one thing there are rules about whom you may choose. For example, a man cannot marry his niece and a woman cannot marry her stepson or her son-in-law.

Your choice of partner is also limited by opportunity. It is quite obvious that before you can fall in love and marry someone you need to meet them, or communicate in some way. It takes time to get to know someone. You will probably marry someone who goes to the same places that you go to and who you get to know over a period of time. 'Love at first sight' is alright for the storybooks. In real life your partner is likely to be someone that you meet at school, or college, or at work. They are also likely to share your background and many of your interests.

Falling in love is not the only pathway to marriage. Some marriages are *arranged* by the parents or by a matchmaker. In many parts of the world marriage not only brings together two people, it also brings together two families. There may be land, wealth and status involved. The two families may want a say in how that wealth and status is to be handed on. In an arranged marriage the two families have an influence over the future of the new family.

When people 'marry for love' the love comes before the marriage. In an arranged marriage a couple learn to love one another after marriage. With their experience of married life, and their knowledge of the couple, the parents are in a better position to make a wise choice of partner. Communities in which there are arranged marriages point to Britain's high divorce rate as evidence that 'romantic love' may not always provide a sound basis for marriage.

Weddings

Weddings are always a time for celebration and for making gifts. In many societies the marriage of a young woman to another family meant the loss of someone whose work was greatly needed. It was usual for the groom's family to make a gift of 'bridewealth' to the family of the bride as a form of compensation. Elsewhere the bride's family will pay a dowry of money or animals to the family of the groom as their share of the marriage contract. In Britain gifts are given to the married couple to help them set up their home.

Gifts of money are given at a Hindu wedding.

In all societies a wedding is an important public event. The ceremony is carried out by someone who is licensed to conduct marriages. This may either be a clergyman or other religious leader, or a Registrar of Marriages who performs civil weddings. When a couple marry their

Figure 4.1 Age of Marriage

The number of people who married in every thousand single people, 1983

Men	Women
16–19	
8.5	32.9
20–24	
81.7	125.7
25–29	
108.6	106.5
30–34	
67.8	62.1
35–44	
29.8	26.9

(Source: OPCS *Population Trends*, Spring 1985)

legal position changes. The law gives them responsibilities to each other and they are treated differently by the official bodies like the Tax Inspector.

It is not every couple that chooses to get married. A couple who live together, perhaps with children, but who have not been legally married have a common-law marriage. They do not have the same legal rights as a couple whose marriage is legally registered, though the law does recognise them as married.

Table 4.1   Teenage marriages
(% of persons under 20 marrying in each year)

	Male	Female
1951	2.8	16.9
1956	4.3	22.5
1961	6.9	28.7
1966	9.9	32.5
1971	10.1	31.1
1976	9.8	31.1
1981	7.2	24.0

(Source: *Women and Men in Britain*, Equal Opportunities Commission, 1985, Table 1.3, OPCS)

Questions
1. What is the word we use to describe a system of marriage in which a woman may have only one husband?
2. What is meant by:
   a polygamy? **b** polygyny? **c** polyandry?
3. What will influence the sort of person you might eventually marry?
4. What arguments would you give for and against a system of arranged marriages?
5. What is the difference between bridewealth and a dowry?
6. What kind of gifts are given at a wedding in Britain?
7. Why do you think it is important for weddings to take place in public?

4.2   The family

Although we all know what we mean by a family it is not always an easy thing to describe. Your family may just be you and your mother, or it may include all of your aunts and uncles, cousins, nephews and nieces, as well as your parents and grandparents. Most, though not all, families involve a married couple, children, and a home in which the family live. Many families only involve one or two of these features but they are still families.

Families are made up of a number of generations. Your parents are of one generation, you are part of another. A family of parents and

Figure 4·2 Nuclear and extended families

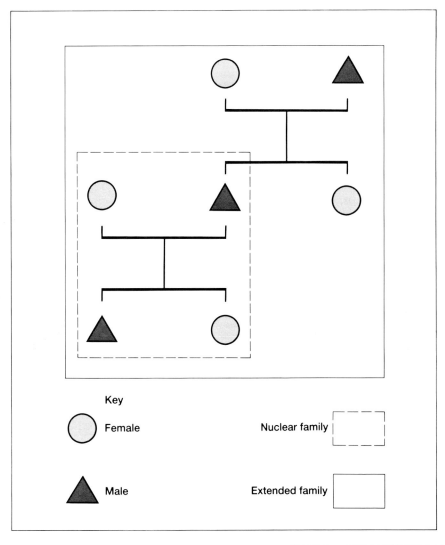

Figure 4.3 Family size, 1976

Number of live births		%
0		9
1		19
2		40
3		23
4 or more		9

(Source: OPCS, 1976)

children has two generations and is called a *nuclear* family. A family which includes grandparents has three generations and is an *extended* family. Every extended family is made up of a number of nuclear families.

The changing family

Two hundred years ago it was quite usual to find families that both lived and worked together. Before the Industrial Revolution the family was an important *unit of production*. Families worked together in their homes to make things for their own use and to sell on the market. The modern industrial economy means that people must go out of their homes to work in factories and offices. The money that they earn is then used to buy things for themselves and their families. The family has changed from a unit of production to a *unit of consumption*.

There have been other changes too. The modern family is smaller than in the past. At the beginning of this century, families with five or six children were quite common. Today families have an average of two children. In 1976 40% of all families had only two children.

Figure 4.4 Working mothers

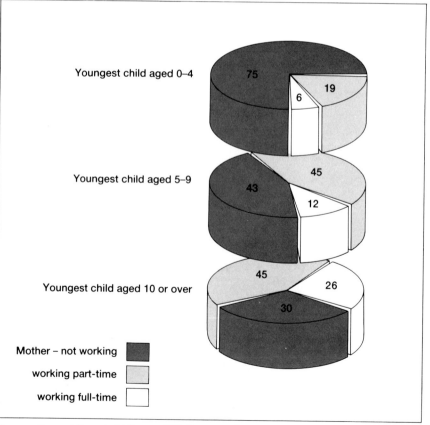

Youngest child aged 0–4

Youngest child aged 5–9

Youngest child aged 10 or over

Mother – not working

working part-time

working full-time

(Source: *General Household Survey*, 1981, Table 4.10)

The nuclear family is often separated from the wider extended family. Whereas at one time most families could easily keep in touch with relatives who lived nearby, now they are more likely to depend on the telephone and the motor car.

Roles within the family have changed also. Although in the past women (and also children) were important wage-earners, it was the man who was considered to be the bread-winner. There is still a widely-held view that 'the woman's place is in the home' and that it is the husband who should go out to work. This is changing. Many families today depend on the wife's earnings. More women are working full-time while the husband shares in the housework and in bringing-up the children. Wives have gained greater equality with their husbands and may follow their own careers whilst also having a family.

CASE STUDY

The kibbutz

When the independent state of Israel came into existence in the 1940s the kibbutzim were set up as an alternative to the family. The children lived in special 'children's houses' looked after by a *metapelet* and only spent a little time each day with their parents. Everyone ate in the community dining room and shared in the daily tasks. Women were not tied to child-rearing and could share in the work of the kibbutz. Men and women could work on the farms and in the factories as equals. Over the years the way of life on the kibbutz has changed. Children now spend more time with their parents within the nuclear family while still remaining as part of the kibbutz.

Questions
1. Can these groups be described as families?
   a A single parent with children
   b A childless couple
   c A common-law marriage with children
   d A couple who have separated and have each taken one of the children
2. What percentage of families had four or more children in 1976?
3. Which of the following statements are true and which are false?
   a Three-quarters of mothers with children under five do not go out to work.
   b Mothers of older children are less likely to work full-time
   c Three out of every ten mothers with children over 10, do not work.
4. What was the name given to the communities which were set up in Israel as an alternative to the family?
5. Make a list of the advantages and disadvantages of the kibbutz way of life.

4.3 A Japanese family

Figure 4·5

N

Sea of Japan

HONSHU

Takashima Osaka •Tokyo

Pacific
Ocean

0 100 km

Japan is a country which has changed very rapidly. The way of life in
a city like Tokyo is very different from life in the countryside.

Hajime Matsui and his wife Hanako live in the fishing village of
Takashima on the island of Honshu in Japan. They have three children.
Hajime's mother and father live with them and his three married sisters
all live in nearby villages. His younger brother, Jiro, has moved away
and now lives in Tokyo. In Japan it is usual for the eldest son to inherit
the family house and to take care of his parents in their old age.

Hanako comes from a village a few miles away. Their marriage was
arranged by the village marriage-broker. She always knew that when
she married she would leave her family and go to live in the home of
her husband's family.

In the summer Hajime fishes for mackerel from the family boat. Hanako
goes with him to help with the nets. When their eldest children, Akira
and Yuriko, are old enough they will help too. Grandmother takes care
of the garden and the orange grove. The mandarin oranges can be sold
on the market to bring in extra money. Grandfather is too old to work.
His eyesight is now so poor that he cannot see to mend the nets and
it would be beneath his dignity to do any other kind of work. He leaves
all of that to his son and to the women.

When Jiro Matsui left the village he knew that there was no future
for him in Takashima. He had been good at school and he won a
scholarship to the University of Kyoto. When he had completed his
studies Jiro found a job with an electronics company in nearby Osaka.

He enjoyed the job and soon gained promotion. He had been working for the company for just over a year when he was called to see Mr Kodama, the manager of his department. Mr Kodama knew that Jiro had no family in Osaka and therefore no-one to arrange a marriage for him. He asked Jiro if he would like to meet his niece, Aki, in the hope that a marriage might be arranged.

Although Mr Kodama arranged their marriage, Jiro and Aki insisted on a long courtship. They wanted to get to know each other before they made the final decision. Their families also had to meet and agree to the marriage.

Soon after the wedding Jiro was moved to Tokyo to work in the head office of the company. They rented an apartment in the suburb of Nerima. Jiro and Aki rarely see their families in Osaka and Takashima. Most of their friends are in Tokyo. They now have a baby daughter.

Questions
1. Draw a family tree to show the extended family of Hajime Matsui.
2. Who inherits the family property in Japan?
3. Who cares for the old people?
4. Why is Hajime's family a unit of production as well as a unit of consumption?
5. Who arranged Jiro Matsui's marriage?
6. Who had to agree to the marriage?
7. Why has the family of Jiro and Aki become isolated from their extended families?

Discussion

In what ways is family life in Takashima and in Tokyo different from family life as you know it in Britain? Use the grid to help you.

Figure 4.6

	Japan	Britain
The extended family is an important part of people's lives		
The family is both a unit of consumption and a unit of production		
Marriages are often arranged		
All of the children of a family share in the inheritance		

4.4 Project: changing families

If you were able to travel back in time to the middle of the eighteenth century you would find many differences in the way families were organised. If you only went back as far as the 1930s you would still find many differences. How great are those differences and can we measure them?

Social scientists have a problem measuring things over time. Some studies do try to follow a particular group of people over a number of years. These are known as *longitudinal* studies. Another approach is to rely on people's memories of how things used to be. This may not always be a reliable source of information but it can be useful. While people's memories give some idea of the past it is more difficult to predict what might happen in the future. The only way to do this is to ask people what they think they will do in 5, 10 or 15 years time. This is no more reliable than using people's memories but does give some indication of how things might be changing.

The survey

The 'changing families' project tries to bring together memories and plans for the future with what is happening now.

Firstly, it collects information from parents, and possibly grandparents, on how things were organised when they were young.

Secondly it uses your own knowledge of family life to collect information on how things are organised today.

Finally, it asks what you think you will be doing in the future. Figure 4.7 shows how you might draw together your results. You will need to use it to design your own questionnaires for each of the three groups. You may wish to change some of the questions or add some more. You may wish to use other populations, elder brothers and sisters, for example.

When you are asking people questions like these you often find that they have far more to talk about than is included on the sheet. An experienced researcher will take a note of any other information that is relevant. It can then be used to make the final report more interesting.

When you have collected your data and have collated it onto the grid you should total the columns and calculate the mean (average) for each heading. Draw your results as a series of graphs.

You can produce your report as a booklet, as a wall display or even as a tape/slide programme.

Figure 4.7

Who does, or did, or do you expect to do these jobs?	In your grandparent's home				In your present home				In your home when you have a family			
	H	W	S	O	H	W	S	O	H	W	S	O
Does the weekly shopping												
Cleans the car												
Changes the baby's nappy												
Arranges the family holiday												
Washes the dishes												
Irons clothes												
Washes the kitchen floor												
Decorates the living room												
Mends fuses												
Mends clothes												
Paints the outside of the house												
Mends the vacuum cleaner												
Puts up shelves												
Buys children's clothes												
Totals												

H   Husband
W   Wife
S   Shared
O   Other

Discussion

1. What different patterns have emerged from your survey?
2. What do the results tell us about changes in family life?
3. Do the results support the idea that there has been a move towards family life in which activities are more equally shared?

4.5   One-parent families

For many people their family is made up of one parent and one or more children. This is a single-parent family, with a lone mother or father. In Britain one in every eight families has a single parent and one in every four children is likely to spend part of their childhood in a one-parent family.

Few families are forever. Families change. A single parent may marry to make a two-parent family. A husband may die leaving a family which now has only one parent. Divorce, separation and re-marriage lead to changing patterns of family life. Many one-parent families only exist for a short time. There are still many people who will have the experience of living in a one-parent family for part of lives.

At one time, if an unmarried woman became pregnant she would feel that she had to get married. This is less likely today. It is now more acceptable for a single woman to bring up children on her own. Unmarried mothers are only a small proportion of all single parents. Over half of all single parents are mothers who have either divorced or separated. Widows make up a further group of single parents. Not all one-parent families have a lone mother. Over one in ten are headed by a lone father.

Figure 4·8 Single parents, 1980

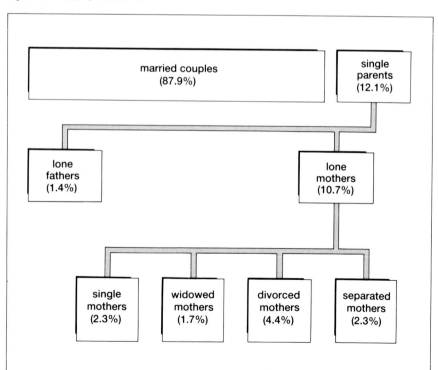

A single-parent often has to do all of the things that are done by a couple in a two-parent family. This often means looking after the home and bringing-up the children and earning a living. The single-parent faces many more problems alone.

One-parent families are, on average, smaller than two-parent families. They are more likely to be living in poor housing and to be dependent on state benefits. Although they are less likely to work than married mothers, when they do lone mothers are more likely to work full-time.

A single parent and his son.

Figure 4·9 Number of dependent children by family type, 1980–81

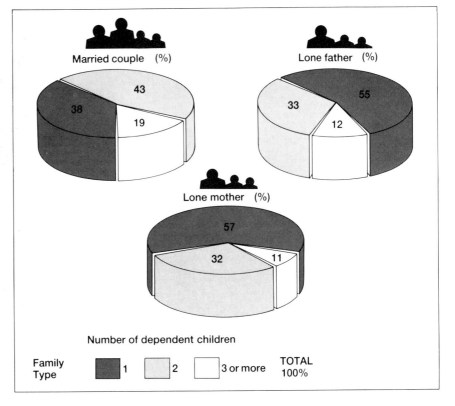

(Source: *General Household Survey*, 1981, Table 2.14)

Poverty and the single parent

'How much poorer are families with only one parent?'
This was one of the questions examined by Peter Townsend in his study of 'Poverty in the United Kingdom'. He used the government's supplementary benefit scales as a measure of poverty.

Figure 4·10 Living conditions of single-parent families

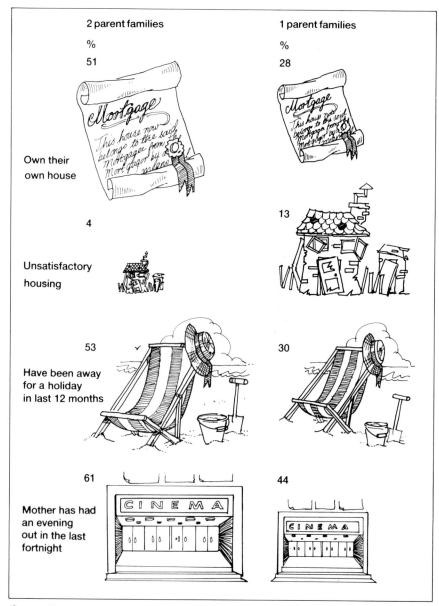

	2 parent families %	1 parent families %
Own their own house	51	28
Unsatisfactory housing	4	13
Have been away for a holiday in last 12 months	53	30
Mother has had an evening out in the last fortnight	61	44

(Source: *Poverty in the United Kingdom* by P. Townsend, 1979 page 769, adapted from Table 22·5)

When he looked at single-parent families as a whole he found that they were worse off than almost any other group. There were, however, very great differences between families. Those families which had a lone father were nearly always better off than those with a lone mother. Widows had a higher standard of living than unmarried mothers. These differences came about because people became single parents at different points in their family lives.

Table 4.2 Poverty and the single parent (1969)

The family income compared to supplementary benefit scales	One-parent families %	Two-parent families %
Less than supplementary benefit level	25	4
Less than twice the supplementary benefit level	55	63
Less than three times the supplementary benefit level	15	24
More than three times the supplementary benefit level	5	8

(Source: *Poverty in the United Kingdom* by P. Townsend, Penguin, 1979, page 760, Table 22.3)

Questions
1. What are the different ways in which someone can become a single parent?
2. Why is it that many one-parent families only last for a short time?
3. What percentage of married couples have three or more children?
4. Why do you think families with a lone father are more likely to have three or more children than families with lone mothers?
5. In what ways are single-parent families at a disadvantage?

4.6 Divorce

Before 1857 divorce was only possible through an Act of Parliament. This meant that there were very few divorces and these were only for the very rich. Since then the law has gradually changed. Our modern divorce laws were introduced in 1969.

Divorce is a legal way of ending a marriage. It is granted by a court when it can be proved that a marriage has broken down completely and there is no chance that the couple might make a fresh start. The law is there to end failed marriages. It also aims to protect the people involved. Special attention is given to the children and to the wife if she is unable to support herself.

At one time it was necessary to prove that there were grounds, such as cruelty or desertion, before a court would allow a marriage to be ended. Today that is no longer the case. If a couple have lived apart for two years and they both want a divorce then the court will grant it.

Separation is an alternative to divorce which does not bring the marriage completely to an end. A separated couple will live apart whilst still legally married. This means that neither partner can remarry. A couple may choose to separate, drawing up a legally binding 'deed of

Figure 4·11 Divorce trends

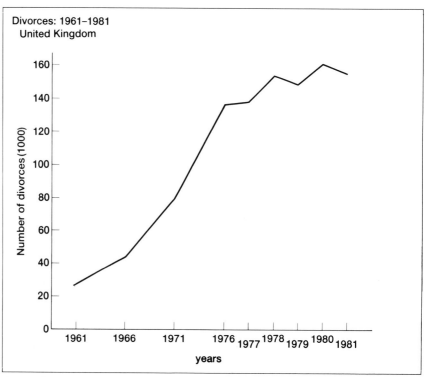

(Source: *Social Trends*, 13 (England and Wales)

separation', or they may be made to separate by a magistrate who grants an 'exclusion order'. This usually happens where there is a danger of violence. Separated couples may decide to give the marriage another try, or may seek a divorce.

If it can be proved that the marriage has broken down, there are no children involved, and both partners want it then the divorce is fairly simple. 'Do-It-Yourself' divorce is possible with only a little help from a solicitor and not much expense. If the divorce is more complicated a solicitor is needed to take care of the legal side. Very often the cost of this is covered by legal aid.

Although divorce is easier to obtain than it has been in the past, it is still a very big step to take. Those who are in favour of easy divorce argue that it is better for a couple to get divorced than for them to continue with a broken marriage. Others argue that it can mean that a couple will use divorce as the easy alternative to trying to make the marriage work.

Divorce trends
Since 1970 there has been a steady increase in the number of divorces each year. It has been estimated that as many as one in three of all marriages since 1981 will end in divorce. Some groups are more likely to become divorced than others. The younger the bride the greater the chance of divorce. For teenage brides one in two marriages will end in divorce. One couple in every thirty divorce after only three years of marriage. Divorce rates are highest for couples aged 25 to 29.

Figure 4·12 Divorce by length of marriage, Great Britain 1981

(Source : *Social Trends*, 13)

Children and divorce

When a couple separate or divorce it is often the children that suffer. In two out of every five divorces no children are concerned. In another quarter of divorces there is likely to be only one child. In those divorces which do involve children it is important to ask whether it is better for children to carry on living in an unsatisfactory home or for the parents to separate.

Figure 4·13 Proportion of divorcing couples with children, England and Wales 1982

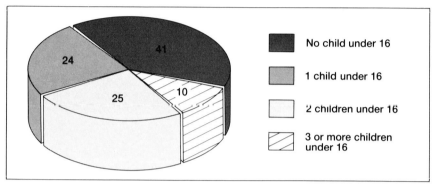

(Source: OPCS)

Figure 4·14 Divorces for every 1000 marriages in Europe

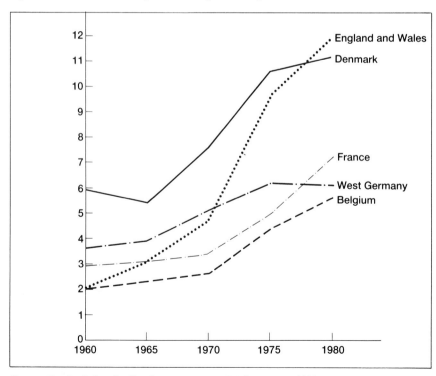

(Source: Family Policy Studies Centre: *Divorce Briefing paper*, 1983, Table 4

Questions
1. What alternatives are there to divorce?
2. What are the arguments for and against easy divorce?
3. What percentage of divorces occur in the first ten years of marriage?
4. In what ways has the pattern of divorce in Britain been different from the pattern in other European countries?

4.7   Vocabulary

Arranged marriage
The marriage has been planned by the parents of the couple, sometimes with the help of a matchmaker. Each family has to agree to the choice of the partner.

Bridewealth
The money, land or animals given by the groom's family to the family of the bride to compensate them for the loss of a worker.

Common-law marriage
A couple who have lived together for a long time, and probably have children, can claim to have a 'common-law marriage'.

Divorce
A legal process which brings a marriage to an end.

Dowry
The wealth given by the bride's family at marriage.

Extended family
A family of three generations including a number of nuclear families.

Family
The social group usually consisting of one or more parents and their children, sharing a common home.

Kibbutz
The type of community set up in Israel as an alternative to the traditional family.

Monogamy
The system of marriage involving one man and one woman.

Nuclear family
The family unit made up of parent(s) and children.

Polygamy
The system of marriage which permits one man to marry more than one woman (polygyny) or one woman to marry more than one man (polyandry).

Separation
A legal process which recognises that a married couple have now parted but have not divorced.

Single-parent family
A family in which there is only one parent, either father or mother. Single-parent families can come about in a number of ways.

CHAPTER 5

LEARNING AND SCHOOLING

We are always learning. As we get older our ideas, knowledge, beliefs and behaviour change. We learn to do new things and gain new skills. Socialisation is one part of that long process of learning while education, training and schooling are others.

Some learning is planned while some just seems to happen. Much of it we do for ourselves but some is done for us, or is done to us. Often we learn something quite different from what was intended. Learning can take place in many different settings, not just in schools.

Learning can take place formally or informally. Formal education takes place in some form of organisation that has been set up to provide it. The education is planned and usually involves people who work as teachers and others who are learners. A school is a good example of somewhere which provides formal education.

Informal education can happen anywhere. It is not planned. It is often difficult to separate it from formal learning. A great deal of informal learning happens in places designed for formal education. Even though the school is part of formal education you learn many things at school which are not on the syllabus and are not always intended.

Learning can take place in many different situations and ways.

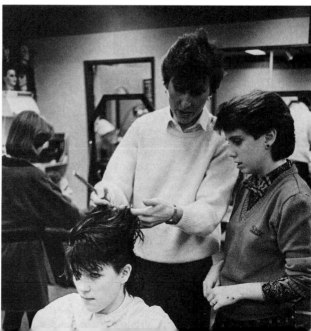

5.1   What are schools for?

Schooling for self reliance

Figure 5·1

Tanzania

Julius Nyerere

Tanzania is a poor country with little industry and few natural resources. Most of its people live by farming. Until 1961 it was ruled by Britain. Its schools were modelled on British schools with the same subjects and the same exams. When Tanzania became an independent nation it needed to create an education system which was more suited to its needs.

Tanzania's leader was Julius Nyerere. He wanted to change the pattern of education. He believed that it only served the needs of the few clever children and did nothing for the mass of the people. Children were not learning things that would be useful in their everyday lives in the villages. The old form of schooling was seen as something separate from people's everyday lives. It made it seem as though the only real education was gained from books. Most importantly it took young people out of the work of the villages at the time when they were most needed.

In 1977 Nyerere introduced a new system of 'Education for Self-Reliance'.

In his plan the schools were to be part of the community and were to prepare children for life in the farming villages. Instead of teaching large numbers of facts that they would never use, the schools were to help children to think for themselves.

To do this the schools were to be based on farms and workshops. In this way children would learn the skills they would need in their lives and it would help the school provide for its own needs. In a country which had very little money to spend on schools this was very important.

The examination system was changed. It was no longer important to select people to go to secondary school or to university. Instead it was to test whether or not the student had gained the education which would be of value to the community.

Nyerere's plan was to make education serve the needs of the nation by developing self-reliance. By this he meant that people should be free to think for themselves and to use their education for the good of all.

Questions
1. Why was the British system of education not suited to Tanzania after independence?
2. Why did Nyerere want to change it?
3. How were the schools changed?
4. How far is 'self-reliance' an important aim in British schools today? How might schools do more to help people to be self-reliant?

Project: what are schools for?

What do people think are the most important aims of the school? This survey was originally carried out with pupils, teachers, parents and school leavers. When all of the replies were added up it became clear that the different groups did not agree about the purposes of school.

Use the questionnaire to conduct a survey in your school. Discuss your findings and write a short paragraph stating your conclusions.

Figure 5.2 What are schools for?

QUESTIONNAIRE

These are a number of things that people have said schools should be doing to prepare young people for adult life.

Do you think they are:

> a very important?
> b fairly important?
> c not at all important?

Circle the number which reflects your view of each statement

	Very important	Fairly important	Not at all important
1. Help them to do as well as possible in examinations	3	2	1
2. Teach them things that will be of direct use to them in their jobs	3	2	1
3. Teach them about different careers and jobs so that they can decide what they want to do	3	2	1
4. Teach them about things that will be useful in running a home, for example, about bringing-up children and home repairs	3	2	1
5. Teach them how to manage their money when they have left school and about things like rates and income tax	3	2	1
6. Help them to become independent and able to stand on their own feet	3	2	1
7. Teach them about what is right and wrong	3	2	1
8. Teach them how to behave so that they will be confident and at ease when they leave school	3	2	1
9. Help them to know what is going on in the world.	3	2	1
10. Give them interests and hobbies that they can do in their spare time	3	2	1

(Source: adapted from Schools Council Enquiry One: *The Young School Leaver*, Schools Council, 1968)

5.2   The development of schooling

Schools for the mass of the people began to appear at the end of the eighteenth century. They were often provided by charities and by the churches. It was not until 1870 that an Act was passed which allowed local 'school boards' to set up their own 'elementary' schools.

These schools were *elementary* because they only provided a basic, or elementary, education. To gain more than this meant going to a *secondary* school. Until 1944 secondary schools only took fee-paying pupils, or those who had won a scholarship.

In the middle of the Second World War the 1944 Education Act was passed. It aimed to provide an education for all children which was suited to their age, aptitude and ability.

Local Education Authorities (or LEAs) were created to control the schools in each area. Younger children were now educated in 'primary schools'. There was 'secondary education for all' through a 'tri-partite system' with three different types of secondary school. At the age of 11+ children took an examination and were selected to go to a secondary school which suited their aptitude (what they were good at), and their ability (how good they were at it).

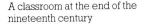

A classroom at the end of the nineteenth century

Figure 5·3 Tri-partite system

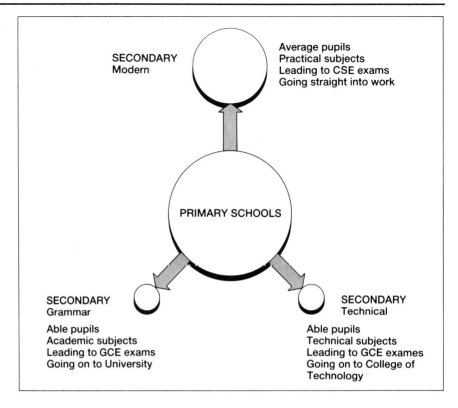

SECONDARY
Modern

Average pupils
Practical subjects
Leading to CSE exams
Going straight into work

PRIMARY SCHOOLS

SECONDARY
Grammar

Able pupils
Academic subjects
Leading to GCE exams
Going on to University

SECONDARY
Technical

Able pupils
Technical subjects
Leading to GCE exames
Going on to College of
Technology

Comprehensive schools

During the 1950s and 1960s more and more people began to see
problems in the way the schools were organised.

The 11+ exam aimed to measure intelligence. It was thought that by
testing a child at eleven years old you could predict how they would
develop. In practice this was not true. Instead of testing a child's
intelligence the 11+ often just tested how good a child was at doing
intelligence tests.

The tri-partite system very soon became a two-school system. Few
of the new secondary technical schools were opened. The grammar
schools became the schools for the successful children and the
secondary moderns were seen as the schools for the failures.

Although many of these schools had second-class status some of the
pupils at the secondary modern schools did as well as many of those
at the grammar schools. People began to realise that something was
wrong with the whole idea of selection at 11+. By separating children
at the age of eleven many were not getting the opportunities they
deserved.

Equality of opportunity became a political issue. The Labour Party
favoured comprehensive schools while the Conservative Party wanted
to keep selection and the grammar schools. There was often strong

Figure 5·4 Comprehensive systems

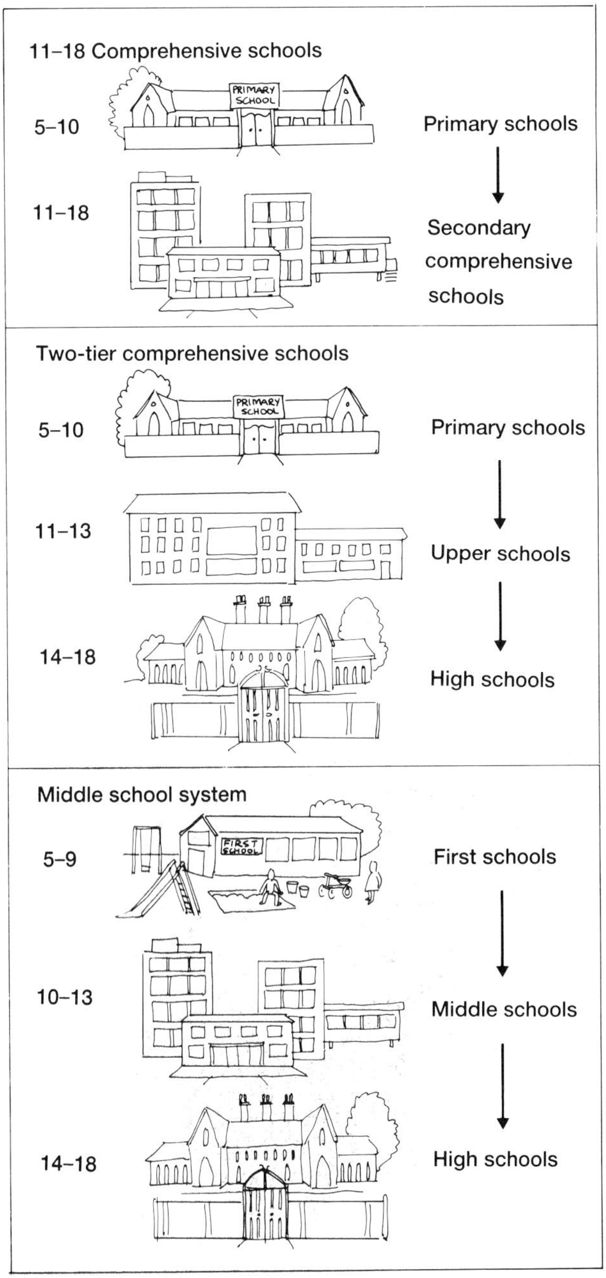

opposition to plans to change the schools.

Despite the opposition, Local Education Authorities began to re-organise on a comprehensive pattern with schools which catered for all children. The new schools took many forms. By 1980 four out of every five children in England and Wales were educated in some kind of comprehensive school.

It was often very difficult to make these schools truly comprehensive. The schools reflected the area from which they drew their pupils. If the neighbourhood was not socially mixed then the school could not be socially mixed either. Even in areas where there was a mix of different social classes, many children were 'creamed-off' to the few surviving grammar schools or to private schools.

Discussion

What are arguments for and against these two views of education:
a There should be one school which caters for all of the children in the area. It should provide them all with the same opportunities and the chance to develop at their own pace.
b Children need to be given an education suited to their individual needs and interests. This can only be done by selecting pupils for separate schools which provide different types of education.

5.3   Education in the eighties

The 1980s were a time of great change in British schools.

For the previous twenty years the schools had been expanding. The birth rate had been rising steadily. More children needed more schools, more teachers, more books and more money. Each year education took a bigger slice of the national income. Eventually the government decided that the growth in spending could not continue. Education's share of the national budget began to fall.

This was partly because the politicians believed that the country could no longer afford to spend so much on schools and colleges. It was also because a fall in the birth rate meant that there were less children to be educated.

Falling school rolls meant less schools and less teachers. Some schools were amalgamated whilst others closed altogether.

Figure 5·5 Pupils leaving school in England

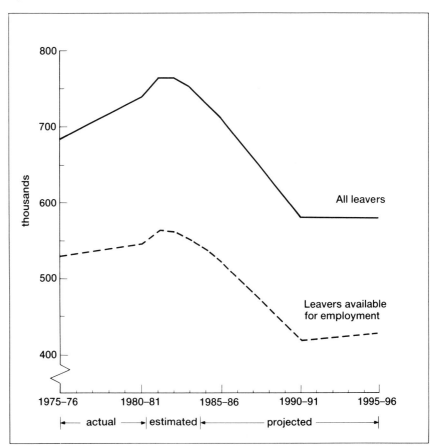

(Source: *DES Report on Education,* no. 97, May 1982)

The great debate

In 1977 James Callaghan, the Labour Prime Minister, spoke at Ruskin College in Oxford. In his speech he introduced a 'great debate' on education. The cost of education and the fall in pupil numbers were only two of the issues that faced the schools. Throughout the 1970s and into the 1980s there had been a growing concern about standards of education, about the content of the school curriculum and about control over what went on in the classroom. In starting the great debate James Callaghan aimed to tackle all three concerns.

During the 1960s there had been many changes in the way school subjects were taught. New approaches to teaching mathematics and English had developed. New subjects such as social science had appeared on the school timetable. In primary schools there was a move towards 'child-centred' learning which allowed children greater freedom to develop at their own pace.

Figure 5·6

(Source: *The Sun*, 23 March 1986)

" MUST BE TIME FOR MATHS ! "

There was a fear that these changes would cause standards to fall. These fears were given publicity in a series of 'Black Papers' and were taken up by the newspapers. There was very little evidence to support these worries. What evidence there was tended to show that standards were actually rising. Despite this there was strong public feeling that in some way the schools were not doing their job properly.

There was also a concern that the schools were not doing enough to prepare young people for their working lives. School subjects needed to be more 'vocational'. New courses and new examinations were introduced. The Certificate in Pre-vocational Education, or CPVE, was introduced as a qualification which would prepare people for starting work.

For many years the teachers in the schools had been left to organise the curriculum in the way they thought best for the pupils. The great debate changed that. The government began to exercise greater control over what was taught. Parents also gained greater influence as school governors. There were important changes in the control of education.

Project: learning about work

An important issue since the great debate has been a demand for people in school to know more about the world of work. Many schools introduced work experience schemes to provide pupils with this experience.

Young people gain experience of paid work in many ways. Some will have paper-rounds or Saturday jobs. Others will do paid work at home, cleaning the car or babysitting. Sometimes people do these jobs and are not paid. There are different ways of finding jobs, and different reasons for working.

Plan and carry out a survey to discover what experience young people have of 'the world of work'.

5.4   Private education

Figure 5·7

Some parents choose to pay for their children to be educated in private schools. These are sometimes known as '*independent* schools'. Some are run by charities and educational trusts though many are private businesses which aim to make a profit by providing education to those who are prepared to pay for it.

The best known independent schools are called 'public schools', though they are in fact private. Although many of these schools may be able to trace their history back to the sixteenth and seventeenth centuries most of them have only developed in their modern form in the last hundred years. They are mainly schools for boys, although there are a number of girls' public schools. Some boys' schools do allow girls into the older forms. Most are boarding schools whose pupils live in 'houses' attached to the school.

Public schools take pupils at 13. There are 'preparatory' schools which prepare younger pupils for the entrance examinations. As well as fee-paying pupils most schools also take pupils on scholarships and some whose fees are paid by Local Education Authorities. Links between these schools and the universities of Oxford and Cambridge are very close. Many cabinet ministers, top civil servants, leading bankers and directors of large companies were educated at public schools.

The opponents of private schooling claim that independent schools give many people an unfair advantage later in life. It is argued that it is wrong for the nation's leaders to be educated separately from the majority of ordinary children. Those who support such schools claim that parents should have the right to choose how to have their children educated, even if this means that they have to pay for it.

Not all independent schools are 'public schools'. Some independent primary and secondary schools are very similar to state schools and pupils may transfer from one system to the other. Parents choose these schools because they believe that by paying their children will get a better education.

Parents may also wish their children to have a particular kind of education, at a church school for example. Religious groups set up these schools to make sure that children are taught in a way which suits their own faith. There are other schools which provide for children who are very good musicians or dancers. Different nationalities have their own schools, providing an education in their own language or to fit the examination system of their own country.

Pupils at an Orthodox Jewish day school.

Table 5.1   Pupils at private schools (ages 5–18) percentages

Year	Maintained schools %	Direct grant schools %	Independent schools %	Total
1951	90.8	1.4	7.8	100
1956	91.7	1.4	6.9	100
1961	92.3	1.5	6.2	100
1966	92.7	1.6	5.7	100
1971	93.9	1.5	4.6	100
1976	94.3	1.4	4.3	100
1981	93.8	—	6.2	100

(Source: adapted from The Political Arithmetic of Public Schools by A. H. Halsey *et al.* in G. Walford (ed.) *British Public Schools: Policy and Practice*, Falmer Press, 1984)

Questions
1. Why are private schools sometimes called 'independent schools'?
2. Name two public schools.
3. In what ways are public schools different from state schools?
4. Why might parents choose to send their children to private schools?
5. What was the percentage of pupils who attended independent schools in 1951?
6. Did the percentage of pupils in independent schools rise or fall between 1951 and 1976?
7. Why did the percentage of pupils at independent schools appear to rise in 1981?

5.5   Schooling in the USSR

The system of education in the USSR is the largest in the world with over 50 million people involved in full-time education and many more studying part-time.

After the revolution of 1917 Russia's leaders realised that education would be important in building a new society. They therefore created a pattern of education which fitted the ideas and beliefs of the Soviet State.

Children usually start school at the age of seven, though some may attend kindergarten from the age of three. All children go to a general school which serves the area in which they live.

The government's aim has been to provide all children with a full ten-year education, between the ages of 7 to 17. Many young people, however, leave at the end of the eighth year and either continue their education part-time or go on to work and production courses. Some go on to special vocational schools or to one of the secondary specialised schools which provided training for professions such as nurses, technicians and kindergarten teachers. Many go to university.

Inside Soviet schools

The 1st September is an important day in the Soviet Union. It is the day when the new school year begins. The event is marked by speeches and presentations. Children bring bunches of flowers for their teachers. The ceremonies to mark the start of the school year are a sign of the importance attached to education in the USSR.

In appearance, Soviet schools are similar to schools in any industrial country. There are the same classrooms, the same desks, the same teachers and pupils, even the same lessons. It is only when you look more closely that you will begin to see the differences.

The first thing you might notice is the picture of Lenin which hangs in every classroom. There may be posters with slogans stressing the importance of working hard and keeping healthy. These often show children wearing red neckerchiefs, the symbol of the Young Pioneers to which all children of secondary school age belong.

Soviet schools are not only there to give to children the knowledge and skills that they will need later in their lives. They are also concerned with *vospitanie*, or upbringing. An important task of the school is to make its pupils into good citizens, and in the USSR that means good communists.

There are many ways in which 'vospitanie' is carried out by the school. The Soviet way of life places an emphasis on living and working as part of a group or collective. Each class is a unit of one of the communist youth organisations. The youngest children are Octobrists. When they reach the age for secondary school they become Pioneers. At 16 they may join the Komsomol, or Young Communist League.

In school the collective ideal is seen in the shared responsibility that pupils have for the care of the classroom, for the good behaviour of members of the class and for the standards of work.

Soviet education is also *polytechnic*. It is based on the principle that learning from books must always go hand-in-hand with practical work. Within the schools there will often be 'production brigades' and joint projects with local industries. In the summer holidays the Young Pioneers will run camps where young people will help with the harvest or with forestry. For the older pupils there is also compulsory military training for two hours each week.

Figure 5.8

The rules of the Octobrists

1. Octobrists are future Pioneers.
2. Octobrists are diligent, study well, like school, and respect grown-ups.
3. Only those who like work are called Octobrists.
4. Octobrists are honest and truthful children.
5. Octobrists are good friends, read, draw, live happily.

A portrait of Lenin, founder of the Soviet State, looks over a classroom in Ulyanovsk.

5.6   Schools

Schools in countries like the USSR and France are under the direct control of a government department. Education is centralised. The same subjects are taught, at the same time, using the same textbooks right across the country. British schools are not like that. Although the government has an increasing influence over what is taught, it is still left to the school to decide how it will organise its work. Education in Britain is decentralised. Every school is different. It will plan its curriculum to meet the needs of the area and of the children who attend the school.

As well as the formal curriculum in each school there is also a *hidden curriculum* of ideas and attitudes. This is part of the informal learning that goes on within the school. In some schools that informal learning is more important than the lessons that are on the timetable.

CASE STUDY

Summerhill

Summerhill is a boarding school in Suffolk which was started by A. S. Neill in 1921. It is a school which encourages freedom. No one has to go to lessons and there are few rules. There is no homework and no exams. Summerhill is a democratic school. Every Saturday night all of the teachers and pupils meet for a General School Meeting. Everyone from the headmaster down has one vote and all must abide by the majority decisions.

In reply to a parent who had asked if she could visit the school on a particular Monday, Neill once wrote that as they were getting about forty visitors a week the children had made a rule that visitors should only be allowed on Saturdays. If he, as headmaster, broke that rule he would be fined his pudding.

Children who were sent to Summerhill after failing at an ordinary school often suffered from what Neill called 'lesson aversion'. Their dislike of learning was often so great that they would do anything except go to lessons. This sometimes went on for months. It was only when they got their experiences of other schools out of their system that they settled down to work.

Discussion

Compare the kind of education provided by A. S. Neill at Summerhill with the way your school is run. What are the differences? How important are they?

What would children at Summerhill learn informally as part of the 'hidden curriculum'. What is the 'hidden curriculum' of your school?

Classrooms

The hidden curriculum also influences what happens in classrooms. Classrooms are places where some people teach and others learn. Just by looking at a classroom you can gain an idea of how teaching and learning is supposed to happen, and what the roles of teacher and learner mean.

Teachers use different styles of teaching. In one classroom the teacher seems to spend most of the time talking, asking questions and writing on the blackboard. The pupils do a lot of writing and are not expected to say very much. At any one time they are all doing the same work. Here the teacher has a *traditional*, or formal, style of teaching.

In another classroom the teacher moves about between groups of pupils answering questions and checking work. The blackboard is occasionally used to write up a difficult word or to give some homework. The pupils are all working at their own pace so a number of different things are going on at any one time. There is a lot of talking, most of it about the work. In this classroom the teacher has a *progressive* or informal style.

Traditional teaching styles are quite good at helping people to learn information. On the other hand progressive methods are better at helping people think for themselves.

Discussion

Which of the following are typical of formal teaching and which would be found in informal classrooms?
  Which style of teaching do you prefer?

Figure 5.9 Formal and informal classrooms

	Formal	Informal
Pupils work at their own pace		
The teacher is the main source of knowledge		
Pupils work in groups		
Pupils are encouraged to discover things for themselves		
There is a lot of copying from the blackboard		
The teacher makes all of the decisions about what is to be learned		
The pupil's main task is to remember things		
The teacher is there to help pupils and answer questions		
The teacher asks all of the questions		

5.7   Sorting them out

Most schools divide their pupils into various groups. Different groups are treated differently. They may have different lessons, study different subjects and take different examinations. This sorting-out is known as differentiation.

Differentiation

The most obvious sorting-out is by age. For most of your school life you are with people of the same age. Schools do not have to be organised in this way. Classes could be based on 'standards' with all of those who have reached the same level working together. This often happens in Judo clubs or dancing classes.

  Some differentiation is less obvious. Many schools differentiate by gender. Since the 1975 Sex Discrimination Act schools have had to give boys and girls an equal opportunity to take any subject on the school curriculum. There are, however, still subjects in which most pupils are boys and others in which most pupils are girls. Even when boys and girls are together in the same classes they may be treated differently. Teachers often have different expectations of boys and girls.

In most schools there is some form of differentiation by ability. This may be by *streaming* pupils into different classes for all or most of their timetable, or by *setting* them into different classes depending on their abilities at different subjects. As you move through the school you get more choice in what you will learn. When you come to take exams there are usually options. The 'sorting-out' which takes place right through the school is also working here. Age is still important. You can only choose your subjects when you are older. Your sex and ability will also influence what you choose.

Table 5.2   CSE entries for boys and girls, 1984 (Mode 1)

	Number of entries	
Subject	Boys	Girls
Religious studies	25 923	38 790
English	337 070	335 346
French	58 777	103 295
Mathematics	203 593	226 544
Physics	131 016	36 241
Chemistry	66 071	52 390
Biology	66 091	148 735
Technical Drawing	78 916	5 132
Needlework	138	26 444
Social studies	40 338	51 253

(Source: adapted from Statistics of School Leavers, CSE and GCE England 1984, Department of Education and Science, Table C25, HMSO)

Craft is a subject studied by boys and girls.

Motivation

We all know that you work harder at things you enjoy doing and that people learn best when they want to learn. This is motivation and it can be influenced by many things. You should see some point in what you are doing. It should be interesting and well presented. It is even better if it is fun. Doing well at things, and being told that you are doing well, also increases your motivation.

Everyone works better if they feel that they are succeeding or making progress. We like to be rewarded for doing well or trying hard. Many schools have systems of rewards which aim to motivate pupils to work hard. The most important rewards are praise and recognition. If someone we respect tells us that we are doing well we will be more motivated in the future.

Labelling

Teachers have expectations of their pupils. They expect some to do well and others to do not-so-well. How might these expectations influence how well a pupil actually works?

This has been the cause of controversy ever since an experiment by two American psychologists seemed to prove that children did better if their teacher thought that they were clever. It seemed that when teachers 'labelled' pupils as 'bright', or 'slow', or 'troublesome', the pupil's behaviour changed. They behaved in the way they had been labelled.

In reality things are not quite that simple. Labelling on its own will not change how someone behaves. The pupil has first to accept the label that is given. This is more likely to happen if other people, particularly those whose views are accepted, also agree with the label. If the labelling takes place regularly in public the chances of it being accepted are greater. Even so, pupils do have a choice. They do not have to accept the way others see them. They could ignore it altogether or change their behaviour so that the label no longer fits.

5.8   Vocabulary

Comprehensive schools	Secondary schools which take pupils of all abilities.
Curriculum	The school curriculum is made up of all of the subjects and activities which are part of the school timetable. Activities, such as clubs and teams, which are not on the timetable are sometimes said to be 'extra-curricular' or 'outside of the curriculum'.
DES	The Department of Education and Science which is the government department responsible for education.
Differentiation	The process of dividing pupils within the school by age, gender or ability.

Formal education	The education provided through some form of organisation specially set up to provide education.
Hidden curriculum	Those things which are learned at school but which are not part of the formal curriculum and may not even be intended.
IQ	Intelligence Quotient is a measure of intelligence based on certain tests. It has been replaced by other types of measurement which reflect particular abilities.
Independent schools	Schools which are outside of the state system of education and which either charge fees to cover the cost of the schooling or provide scholarships for clever children.
Labelling	Some pupils may be seen in particular ways by teachers and other pupils. They could be 'labelled' as 'idle', 'clever', 'a troublemaker', 'a swot', or 'an ear'ole'. These labels may affect how the person behaves.
LEA	The Local Education Authority is responsible for running the schools in its area. LEA schools are sometimes known as 'Maintained Schools' or 'County Schools'.
Mixed ability	Pupils of all abilities are taught together in the same class.
Motivation	To be well motivated is to want very much to do something, and to do it well. People who lack motivation do not really want to make an effort.
Primary school	Schools which take pupils from 5 to 11, often in separate infant and junior departments. They were introduced in the 1944 Education Act to provide an elementary education. In some parts of Britain they are called 'first schools'.
Secondary school	Schools which take pupils from 11 to 16 or 18 and prepare pupils for work or for further education at college or university. They may be comprehensive or selective.
Setting	Pupils are separated into groups for particular subjects on the basis of their ability in that subject.
Streaming	Pupils are separated by their general ability into groups which have all of their lessons together. When there are a number of groups of the same level of ability it is called 'banding'.
Syllabus	In each school subject there is a syllabus which lays down the skills, knowledge and activities which will be covered by that subject. Examination syllabuses lay down the material that must be covered for that exam.

CHAPTER 6 INDUSTRY AND TRADE

In a simple farming community each family will produce just enough for its own needs. There will be little left when these needs have been met. Any surplus will be traded for other things the family cannot produce for itself. People work for themselves and see the results of their own work. They usually own the land that they farm and the tools that they use.

In an industrial society people must produce more than they themselves need. They must produce a *surplus* which can be used in trade. The money that is gained in this way can then be used to buy raw materials and to pay the workers. The workers seldom own the land or the tools that they use.

Few people work for themselves. They usually work for an employer who owns the means by which the workers can produce and who organises production. The employer, who is sometimes known as the capitalist, buys the raw materials, sells the finished products and pays the workers, keeping some money back as profits.

This organisation of production into firms and industries, with employers and employees, wages and prices is an important feature of industrial societies. It has an influence on every aspect of social life.

6.1   The pattern of industry

People work at many different jobs and use different skills.

Manual workers work with their hands, needing physical strength and skill in making or doing things. They are sometimes called *blue-collar* workers. Non-manual work requires skills in organising and in dealing with 'paper-work', or with people. Non-manual workers are sometimes known as *white-collar* workers.

As well as working in different jobs, people work in different industries. Some of these industries produce objects, such as washing machines, cars and packets of cornflakes. The things they make are often described as *products* or *goods*. Some goods and raw materials are taken directly from the land, either by mining or by farming. This is done by *primary industries*. Manufacturing industries use raw materials to produce goods and are known as *secondary industries*.

Not all raw materials come from primary industry. Some are produced by other secondary industries. Finished products may either be sold to consumers or used by other producers to help them to make yet more products.

As well as industries which produce goods there are also many industries which provide services. These services may include hairdressing, selling houses, arranging insurance, cleaning windows,

Figure 6·1 Chain of distribution

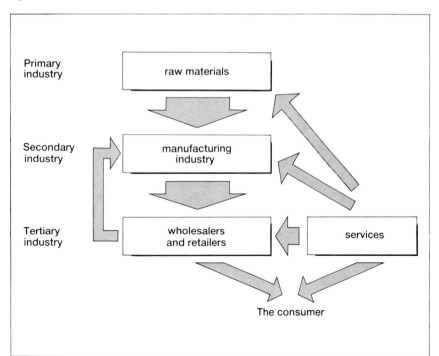

mending cars and many other things. Industries which provide services are sometimes called *tertiary industries*.

An important part of service industry is concerned with commerce. This includes banking and insurance as well as the distribution of goods produced by manufacturers. The shops in the High Street are at the end of a long chain of distribution which stretches right back to the factories where goods are made.

Industrial change

At the beginning of this century iron and steel making, shipbuilding and heavy engineering were the major industries in Britain. Textiles, especially making cotton goods, were also important. Most of these industries were based in the North of England, in the Midlands and in Scotland. Britain's wealth depended upon the export of manufactured goods to the rest of the world.

These older industries were based on coal, iron and steam. The new industries which developed in the twentieth century were based on oil, plastics and electricity. These industries could be placed anywhere in the world and did not need to be near to coalfields or supplies of iron. The pattern of industry in Britain was forced to change.

As the older industries have become less important new industries have taken their place. The motor industry developed in the 1920s and 1930s. Industries which turned oil or coal into plastics and chemicals took the place of the traditional heavy industries. The production of electrical equipment and the making of goods for the home developed rapidly. Instead of being in the industrial North of the country these industries developed in the Midlands and the South where there was a good supply of labour.

By the 1970s these industries also began to change. New products, based on computers and electronics, used new technologies. It was often cheaper to produce these goods in Japan and the Far East from where they could be shipped anywhere in the world.

In Britain fewer people worked in production and more people worked in service industries. Britain was still an important manufacturing nation which exported its goods all over the world. More of its wealth, however, began to come from North Sea oil and from the *invisible export* of services such as insurance and banking.

Figure 6·2 Industrial change

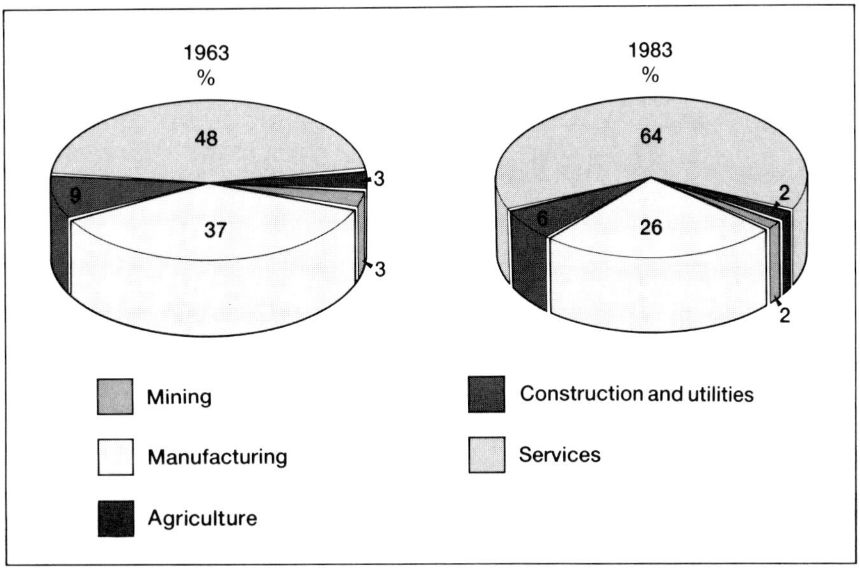

(Source: Adapted from *Employment Gazette* and *The State of the Nation*
by S. Fothergill and J. Vincent, Pluto Press, 1985)

Questions
1. Give examples of:
    a a primary industry
    b a secondary industry
    c a service industry
2. Many manufactured goods are bought by consumers. How else
    might they be used?
3. In what ways has British industry changed since 1900?
4. Which service industry had the greatest increase in the number
    of workers employed between 1961 and 1981?
5. What effects might these changes in the importance of different
    industries have on:
    a areas of the country where coal-mining and steel-making were
    the main industries?
    b the job opportunities open to school leavers?
    c the subjects that it would be important to study at school?

6.2   Production

Factors of production

Figure 6·3 Factors of production

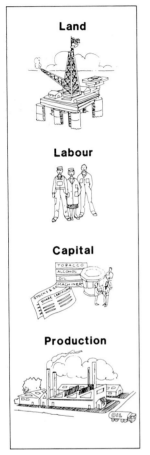

A firm's profit is the difference between what it costs to make the goods or to provide the services and what it receives as income from sales or government subsidies. The costs of production come from the three *factors of production.*

The first of these factors of production is *land.* When economists use the term 'land' they mean more than the land on which a factory is built. Land includes all of those things which come from the land in some way. These include the raw materials from which the finished goods are produced. Raw materials are often a large part of the costs of production.

The second factor of production for which the firm must pay is *labour.* Labour is used to turn the raw materials into finished products. It increases the value of the raw materials. When a potter turns a lump of clay into a bowl, value is added to the clay. It is worth far more as a bowl than it was worth as clay. The workers sell their labour power to the factory owners and in return they receive wages or salaries.

The third expense for the firm is the cost of its *capital.* Factories, machines, stocks of raw materials and unsold goods are part of the capital of a firm. Firms will borrow money to provide them with capital and must then pay interest on the money that has been borrowed.

Production

When a craftsman makes a piece of furniture he begins with an idea of how the finished product will look. A pattern is made. The wood is cut and shaped. When all of the parts have been assembled it is sanded and polished ready for use. At one time *craft production* was the usual way to produce things. As a method of production it depended upon the skill of the craftsman. Tools and machines might be used but they could not take the craftsman's place.

In some craft industries the process of production might be divided into a number of stages. Less skilled workers would carry out the simpler processes, leaving the craftsman to do the skilled work.

When factories began to be set up in the eighteenth century the methods of production began to change. The process of manufacture was divided up into many different stages each requiring much less skill. Each worker would carry out one small part of the process. This is known as the *division of labour.*

Machines performed the most difficult tasks, making it possible for the factory owner to replace the skilled craftsmen with workers who were less skilled and less well paid.

In a modern factory machines are an essential part of production. They cut, shape, join, weigh or mould the objects being made. The workers feed the machines with unfinished parts and then pass the machined pieces on to the next stage in the process. The pace of work is often controlled by the machine. Workers are paid by piece rates according to the amount that they produce in a day or in a week.

A car body moving through the washer before being prepared for painting.

Location of industry

Industries do not grow up in particular areas by accident. A factory owner will set up a factory in the place which gives the best advantages. It could be near to raw materials or near to the market. It may be important to have other firms in the area with a trained experienced work force and suppliers of specialist goods and services. Much depends on the product which is being made and the costs of transport. Firms are set up and factories are built in places where the costs of production are lowest. Factories may be moved when lower costs can be found elsewhere. In many parts of the country firms may receive help from local agencies as an encouragement to set up a factory and bring jobs to the area.

Project

Carry out a survey on industry in your local area. Which kind of industry is most common – primary, secondary or service industry? Which industries are the largest employers? What kind of production methods are used? What qualifications do employers look for in new entrants?

6.3   Technology at work

Tools have been used since people first used pieces of flint to shape arrow heads. Machines are tools which provide workers with greater power and accuracy. With machines it is possible to produce large numbers of identical parts. The different parts can then be assembled. This forms the basis for mass production.

The first factories contained a number of separate machines each carrying out one stage in the production process. Factory owners soon realised that it would be more efficient if the machines were joined together in some way. The parts would move from one machine to the next in a continuous line. Many factories are now organised around *assembly lines.* The line or 'track' moves the products slowly along from one group of workers to the next. At each stage more parts are added. The finished product comes off at the end of the line. This form of mass production can be used to make anything from cars to cream cakes.

Assembly lines cannot be used to make every type of product. Some things, ships and aeroplanes, for example, are too big. Before manufacturers set up production lines, with all of their specialised tools, they need to know that it is worth the expense. If only a small number of items is to be made, or if the product keeps changing, then other methods might be cheaper. *Batch production* is used to produce a 'batch' of one product before the machines are re-set to produce a 'batch' of something else.

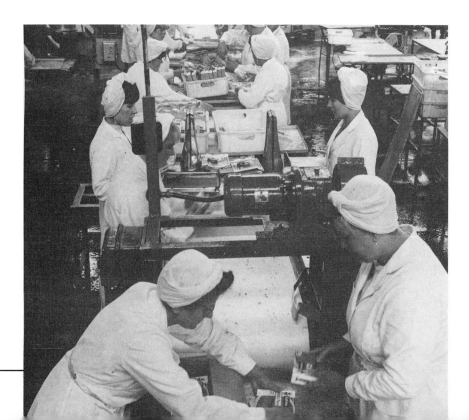

Automation

In a modern factory machines do more than make things. They are also able to control other machines. This can be as simple as using a device to count the number of items produced and then to control the speed of the machine. It can also mean a car factory in which computers control the flow of engines and car bodies which are assembled into motor cars by automated robots.

In some factories *automation* means that raw materials are fed in at one end and the finished product comes out at the other. Oil refineries are one example of this type of *process production*.

Automation relies on computers. They make it easier for the manufacturer to control the work flow, to check the finished products and to control the machines. Robots controlled by computers can work in places where human workers would not be safe.

Automation cuts the cost of making things. This helps to make firms more competitive and increases their profits. When production is automated workers may have to re-train or lose their jobs. If a skilled job is automated it can be done by workers who are less skilled. The job becomes *de-skilled*. Automation means that new skills are needed. They are often in jobs like computer programming and electronics.

Firms will also use automation to improve the working conditions of their workers. People often have to work in very unpleasant conditions. Some processes involve great heat or nasty fumes. Robots do not mind the heat or the fumes. They can work anywhere.

Discussion

The effects of technology at work can be put under a number of headings. Give an example for each effect. Can you think of any other headings?

Figure 6.4

Technology reduces the costs of making things	
Technology increases the employers control over the workers	
Technology makes production more efficient	
Technology takes away the need for skill	
Technology improves working conditions	

6.4   Simulation: where to go?

The Tudor Reproductions Co-operative manufactures copies of antique furniture. The co-op began ten years ago when a group of unemployed cabinet makers got together to start their own business. Most of their sales are in the south and south-east of England. The co-op has established a name for itself in the field of antique reproductions and business has grown considerably. Most of the growth has been in the sale of furniture made from imported hardwoods, especially mahogany.

Recently the firm has been approached by a large furniture store in Manchester which wants to market the furniture in the north-west. This order means that production will need to be increased considerably. The old factory in the centre of London which the co-op took over when they started is already too small. This new order means that new premises must be found.

Where should they go?

Figure 6·5

West Purlington Development Agency

Dear Sir,
The development agency was established five years ago to provide employment and new opportunities in this area of the North-West of England. We are able to offer a number of suitable units from £32.50 a square metre including rent and rates, ready for immediate occupation. The agency's Development Programme also provides low-cost finance towards the cost of erecting purpose-built accommodation specially suited to your own needs.
Our location, on the site of a former docks and steelworks, provides excellent road and rail transport to most parts of the country. The re-developed port facilities also provide an ideal route for imported raw materials and for access to world markets.
Being so close to a large urban area provides many advantages. The people of this area are known for their skills and their hard-work. It is usually possible to meet most of a new employer's labour requirements. Grants are also available for the establishment of training courses when required.
The development of worker co-operatives was a central part of the West Purlington Development Plan. As a result we have established a close understanding of the needs of co-operative ventures.
I enclose details of a number of sites which are

Bartingwell Enterprize Park

Dear Sir,

Thank you for your enquiry regarding factory accommodation for the production of furniture. We have a range of suitable factory units ready for immediate occupation. Rents run from £30.00 per square metre.

The Enterprise Park of 120 hectares is built on the site of a disused sewage treatment plant to the north-west of London. It was granted full enterprise zone status in 1983. As you will no doubt appreciate this brings the advantages of exemption from local rates and considerable tax relief. Planning rules have been greatly simplified and as an importer you will also have the benefit of priority treatment by Customs and Excise.

Although the area has no tradition of furniture manufacture there is a good supply of enthusiastic workers who are keen to develop the new skills you might require.

The Park is within easy reach of the M1, M4 and M25 motorways and only a short distance from Heathrow airport. An increasing number of firms are moving into the area and...

MINDELBOROUGH NEW TOWN CORPORATION

Dear Sir,

I am very pleased that you have decided to join the growing number of firms who are considering a move to the heart of the English countryside.

As well as a wide selection of factories at reasonable rents, Mindelborough offers some of the finest modern housing set in one of the most delightful rural areas in the West of England. There is a well-established shopping centre with all of the major stores. Recreational facilities will be further improved later this year with the opening of the Astro-dome sports complex.

Industrial rents start from £27.50 a square metre plus a furher £8.50 per square metre for rates.

For many years now the area has been famous for the design and production of furniture. Some of the best-known furniture manufacturers are located nearby and the local technical college provides specialist courses in the furniture trades. Although unemployment in the area is not high we would not expect you to have difficulty in recruiting suitably qualified workers.

The enclosed brochure will, I hope, give you an idea of

6.5 Firms

Within each industry there are many firms. Most firms are fairly small, though a number of firms are very large indeed. Small firms are often owned and operated by one person, known as a *sole trader*, or by a small group of people who form a partnership.

In a *partnership* each partner takes a share of the firm's profits and a share of the risks. Partners and sole traders are personally responsible for the debts of the firm. Should they be unable to pay the bills, the partners could have to sell their own possessions to raise the money. Their liability for the firm's debts is unlimited.

If the owners of a large business had 'unlimited liability' no one would be prepared to take on the risks involved. Instead large firms are organised as companies with *limited liability*. These must be legally registered under the Companies Act. Companies are owned by shareholders who invest their money in shares of the company. By having 'limited liability' the owners, or shareholders, are only liable for the amount of money they have invested. If the firm goes bankrupt they lose their money but do not have to pay all of the firm's debts out of their personal possessions.

A small private company may have only a few hundred shares. They will often be owned by the members of a family. The shares can only be sold with the agreement of the other shareholders. A large public company would have many thousands of shares which together would be worth millions of pounds. As well as owning a share of the company the shareholders also receive a share in the profits of the firm. This is known as a *dividend*. The shareholders elect a Board of Directors who run the firm on their behalf.

The most important shareholders in many firms are insurance companies and trusts. These are institutional investors. They invest the money that other people have saved. This means that many ordinary people have a small share in many different companies.

Companies are often owned by other companies. Many are owned by foreign investors or by other *multi-national* companies. The government is also a shareholder in many companies as well as being responsible for the big national corporations like British Rail and the National Coal Board.

The floor of the London Stock Exchange is where shares have traditionally been bought and sold. Today most of the trading is done by computer.

Figure 6·6   It is not unusual for the same people to be on the Board of Directors of a number of different companies

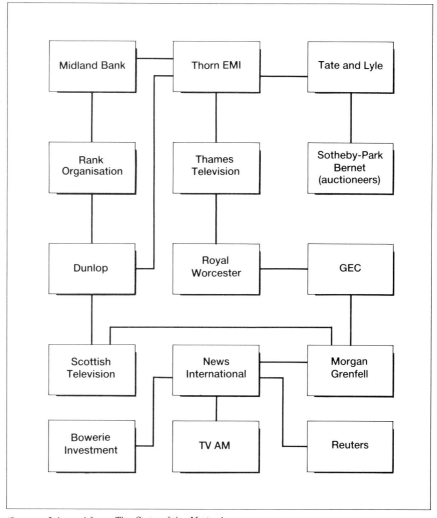

(Source: Adapted from *The State of the Nation* by S. Fothergill and J. Vincent, Pluto Press, 1985)

Shares can be bought and sold on the Stock Exchange. Whilst some buyers want to invest in shares because of the dividends they will earn, others buy in the hope that share prices will rise and they can sell at a profit. This is known as speculation.

Firms can be owned by their own workers. These are the *co-operatives*. A company may provide some of its own shares for its workers or be owned completely by them. In a co-op the workers have a say in how the company is run, they can appoint the managers and have a share in the profits. Co-operatives are usually fairly small businesses producing or selling goods that cannot easily be obtained from larger companies.

6.6   Mergers and takeovers

Firms exist to make profits for their shareholders. To do this they must be able to produce goods and services as cheaply as possible.

Larger firms can often produce things more cheaply than smaller firms. They can make *economies of scale*. They can afford to use machines to manufacture the products. Their overheads can be spread over a larger output of goods. A larger firm can buy larger quantities of raw materials often at special prices.

Many large firms have grown from quite small beginnings. Firms can become larger by joining with other firms. In a merger two companies agree to join together and form a new, larger company. A takeover occurs when one firm gains control of another by buying a majority of its shares.

Competition with other firms forces companies to keep their prices low. They will often try to reduce competition by taking over rival firms. This gives them a larger share of the market and more control over prices. If a firm can take over all of its competitors it has a *monopoly*. This gives it complete control over the supply of the product. Parliament has passed laws which limit the powers of monopolies.

When firms which produce similar products join together it is described as *horizontal integration*.

As well as seeking to reduce competition firms may also want to gain more control over their suppliers and over the outlets for their goods.

A manufacturer may depend on particular suppliers for raw materials. If the supplier raises the price or is unable to supply the goods then the firm could be forced out of business. Greater control may be gained by taking over the suppliers. A manufacturer may also want to control its outlets by taking control of the firms to which it sells its products. This type of amalgamation is known as *vertical integration*.

As well as giving more control over their business, mergers may also enable firms to move into new activities. Companies always look for the best way to make a profit on their capital. They may decide that this can be done by moving into new areas of business, often with little connection to their traditional interests. This is known as *diversification*.

The mergers and takeovers of the last twenty years have led to a smaller number of large companies, each of which has interests in many different areas. Some firms have become very large, employing tens of thousands of workers, some have become multi-nationals. They are often controlled by other companies, with their head offices elsewhere in the world. Some multi-nationals are wealthier and more powerful than many nations.

Figure 6·7 Unilever and its associated companies

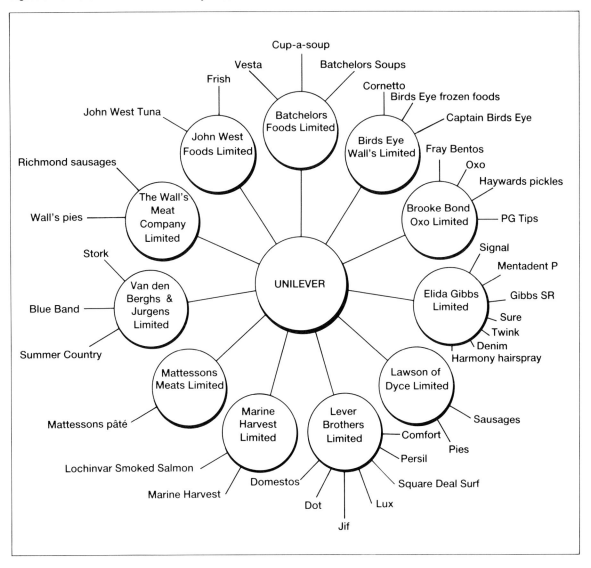

As well as an increase in the size of companies there has also been an increase in the size of the average factory. Although most factories employ less than 200 workers most workers are found in factories which employ far more than 200 people. These changes have had the effect of increasing the distance between the workers and the bosses. The factory worker may never see the directors of the company or even know who they are.

Figure 6·8 Employees by size of factory

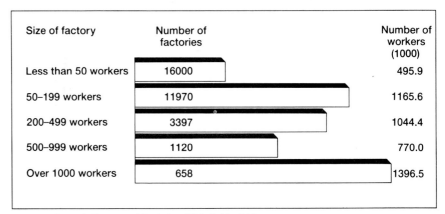

Size of factory	Number of factories	Number of workers (1000)
Less than 50 workers	16000	495.9
50–199 workers	11970	1165.6
200–499 workers	3397	1044.4
500–999 workers	1120	770.0
Over 1000 workers	658	1396.5

(Source: *Annual Abstract of Statistics*, 1985, Table 6·16)

Questions
1. What is meant by:
   a vertical integration?
   b horizontal integration?
   c diversification?
2. Why can a larger company often produce goods more cheaply?
3. Using the information in Figure 6.8, which of the following statements are true and which are false?

Figure 6.9

	True	False
Most factories employ over 1000 people		
There are more workers in smaller factories		
Most workers work in factories employing between 50 and 500 people		
Most factories are fairly small		
The majority of factories employ less than 200 people		

CASE STUDY

6.7 Mondragon

Figure 6·10

When Don Jose Maria Arizmendi came to be parish priest of Mondragon in 1941 the effects of the Spanish Civil War were still being felt.

The town was dominated by one company, the Union Cerrajera, which provided most of the work and ran the only technical school. When the company refused to take on more young men as apprentices Don Jose Maria decided that he must set up a technical school of his own. With the help of the local people the new school was soon taking its first students.

The link with the community was strong and the students spent their time in fund-raising and working for the local people as well as studying. The close link which developed did not end when their training was over and the first group of students went to work at the factory. In Arizmendi's technical school, students and teachers worked together and shared in the day-by-day running of the school. The ideas of co-operation, which had been part of life in the school, were not liked by the factory managers and soon five of Arizmendi's students decided to set up in business on their own.

This was to be no ordinary business. They called their firm ULGOR, from the first letters of their names. It was organised as a co-operative and was the start of the Mondragon experiment. By 1979 there were 135 co-operatives in and around the town. They employed over fifteen thousand workers.

At the centre of the Mondragon worker co-operatives is the 'Caja Laboral Popular', or People's Saving Bank. This is a co-operative bank, owned by its customers. It provides the money to set up the co-operatives and makes sure that they are properly run. Each new co-operative must agree to follow certain rules.

Every co-operative must have an 'open door' to new workers. Anyone for whom there is a job must be able to join the co-operative on payment of a small sum of money. All workers are paid a wage and share in the profits at the end of each year. No one is allowed to earn more than three times the lowest wage. The co-op is run democratically by a Supervisory Board elected by the members.

The Supervisory Board are like the board of directors of a normal company. They appoint the managers and take responsibility for running the firm. The General Assembly of all co-operative workers meets once each year. The workers and managers are represented by the Management Council and the Social Council which give advice to the Supervisory Board. A Watchdog Council watches over all aspects of a co-op's work.

The Mondragon co-ops begin in different ways. Some, like ULGOR, started when a number of people saw a need for a new co-operative. Others developed as offshoots of existing co-operatives or were set up

by the Caja Laboral Popular. Existing co-operatives may also decide to join Mondragon or private firms decide to become co-ops.

Figure 6·11

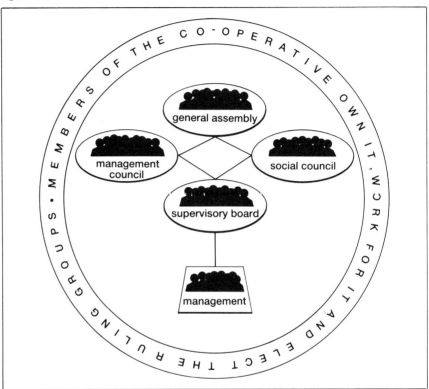

As well as the manufacturing co-operatives there are a number of second-level co-ops. These provide services for the other co-ops. There are housing co-operatives and Alecoop, a co-operative training school which runs its own co-operative factory. Club Arkitle in Bilbao is a co-operative sports and social club while Auzo-Lagun is a women's co-operative providing work for women with young families.

Mondragon's success is partly due to the strong sense of community in northern Spain. It has also been a result of the help and guidance given by the Caja Laboral Popular. The co-ops have also been kept small enough for those who work in them to get to know everyone else.

Discussion

Any successful co-operative must be able to solve four problems:
a Where does the money come from to start the co-operative?
b How can the workers have a say in the way the co-operative is run without everyone getting involved in the day-to-day management?

> c How can new members join if the co-operative is a success?
> d How are the members to be paid a fair wage?
> 1. How did the Mondragon co-operatives solve these problems?
> 2. Imagine that you are about to set up a co-operative to make and
>   sell a product in your local area. How would you tackle the four
>   problems?

6.8 Vocabulary

Blue-collar
A blue-collar worker is someone who is in a manual job, for example, working a machine in a factory.

Capital
A factor of production that is made up of the factories, machines, and other items which are used to produce goods.

Capitalist
Someone who owns capital. Often used to describe the owners of factories or those who employ others to produce goods.

Consumer
Any person or firm who consumes (or uses) goods or products.

Co-operative
A firm that is owned either by its customers or by its workers.

De-skilling
Machinery can take over skilled work and cause the workers to become 'de-skilled'.

Division of labour
The system by which any task or process is divided into a number of stages, each performed by a different group of workers.

Domestic industry
Production of goods in the home either for sale or for an employer or capitalist.

Economy of scale
Firms can often produce goods more cheaply if they produce them in larger quantities, or on a large scale.

Factors of production
The different types of activity or commodity which are needed if firms are to produce goods. They are normally referred to as land, labour and capital.

Investment
Money that is used to finance production. It is used to pay for the firm's capital. Investors usually receive a dividend on the money they invest.

Labour
A factor of production that is made up of the people who sell their time and skills in order to produce goods and services.

Land
The factor of production that includes both the land on which the factory is built and also raw materials used to produce.

Overheads
Those costs that a firm must meet whether or not it produces anything. This includes the interest on loans, rates on the factory and many other 'fixed' costs.

Partnership
A firm consisting of two or more 'partners' who share the risks and the profits.

White-collar
A white-collar worker is someone who works in an office job.

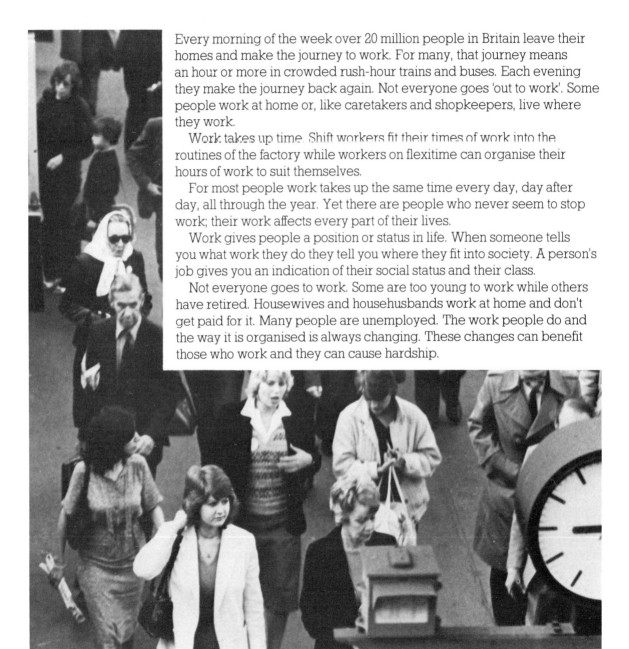

CHAPTER 7

WORK AND LEISURE

Every morning of the week over 20 million people in Britain leave their homes and make the journey to work. For many, that journey means an hour or more in crowded rush-hour trains and buses. Each evening they make the journey back again. Not everyone goes 'out to work'. Some people work at home or, like caretakers and shopkeepers, live where they work.

Work takes up time. Shift workers fit their times of work into the routines of the factory while workers on flexitime can organise their hours of work to suit themselves.

For most people work takes up the same time every day, day after day, all through the year. Yet there are people who never seem to stop work; their work affects every part of their lives.

Work gives people a position or status in life. When someone tells you what work they do they tell you where they fit into society. A person's job gives you an indication of their social status and their class.

Not everyone goes to work. Some are too young to work while others have retired. Housewives and househusbands work at home and don't get paid for it. Many people are unemployed. The work people do and the way it is organised is always changing. These changes can benefit those who work and they can cause hardship.

7.1   Working in Britain

The Labour Force Survey

The Labour Force Survey is carried out every two years. It is a large national survey based on a sample of over 100 000 households in the United Kingdom. The survey provides information on many aspects of employment. It is an important secondary source for social scientists who are studying the working life.

When social scientists carry out surveys they spend much of their time collecting the information. It is only when the information is collected that they can begin to organise it. When studies are based on secondary sources the information is already available. The main task is to organise it in a way which answers the questions you want to ask.

Use the data from the Labour Force Survey to prepare a report on 'Working in Britain'. Your report could take the form of a written project or a wall display. To make it more interesting you may want to use graphs and bar-charts. You could also collect pictures, use interviews and find other information.

Getting started

It is often useful to start a project with a 'map' of the topic you want to study. This can show you the main areas and how they link together.

Figure 7·1

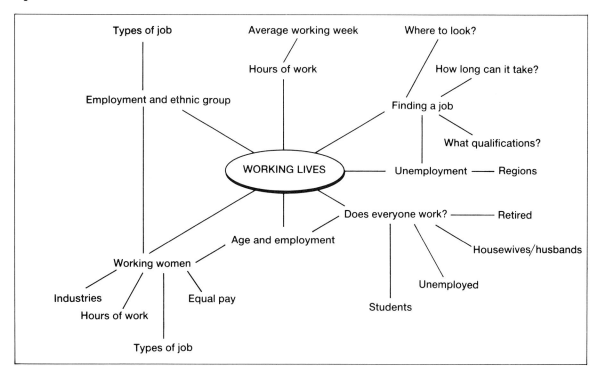

Key questions

When you have worked out the main areas which you want to cover it is helpful to decide on the key questions which you will consider. These may also be used as the sections or chapters of your final report.

Questions you might want to consider could include:

1. How do people get jobs? What qualifications do people have? Is it easier in different parts of the country?
2. Is employment for women different from men's employment? Do they do different jobs? Do they work in different industries?
3. In what ways does race affect employment? What are the implications?

Table 7.1 Working and not working

%	Men	Women	All
In employment	55.4	33.9	43.4
Unemployed	5.9	3.3	4.6
Retired	11.4	11.9	11.7
Housewife	0.2	25.6	13.2
Student	2.9	2.4	2.6
Aged under 16	23.8	21.3	22.5
Others, (including sick and disabled)	2.4	1.3	2.0
Total	100	100	100

(Source: adapted from *Labour Force Survey 1981*, OPCS, Table 4.3)

Table 7.2 Looking for work

	Number of months looking for work		
	Less than 1 month %	More than 3 months %	More than 12 months %
Northern England	7	80	51
Yorkshire and Humberside	7	77	49
East Midlands	11	74	41
East Anglia	9	73	32
South-East England	10	71	38
South-West England	12	73	34
West Midlands	6	82	52
North-West England	6	81	53
Wales	6	79	50
Scotland	9	78	51

(Source: adapted from *Labour Force Survey 1984*, OPCS Monitor LFS 85/2, Table 2)

Figure 7·2 What job?

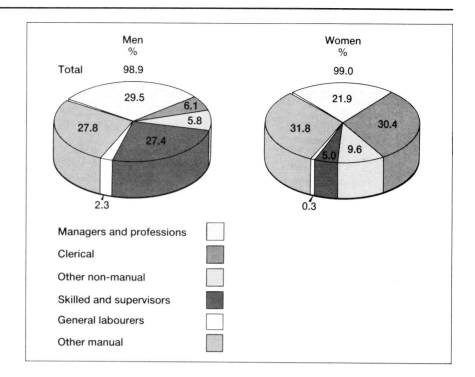

Managers and professions

Clerical

Other non-manual

Skilled and supervisors

General labourers

Other manual

(Source: Labour Force
Survey, 1981)

Figure 7·3

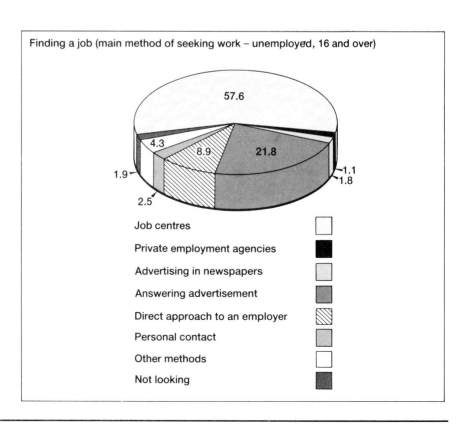

(Source: Labour Force
Survey, 1981)

Figure 7·4 Occupation and ethnic group

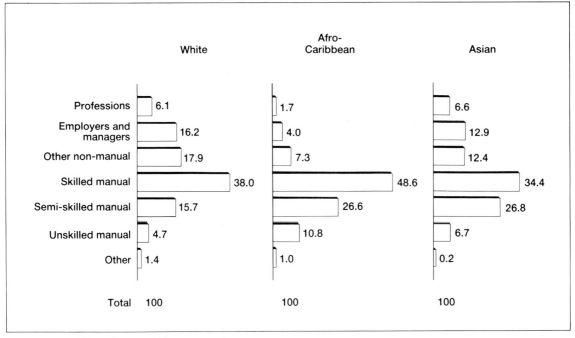

(Source: Labour Force Survey, 1981)

Figure 7·5 Length of time spent seeking work by 16–19 year olds, 1983

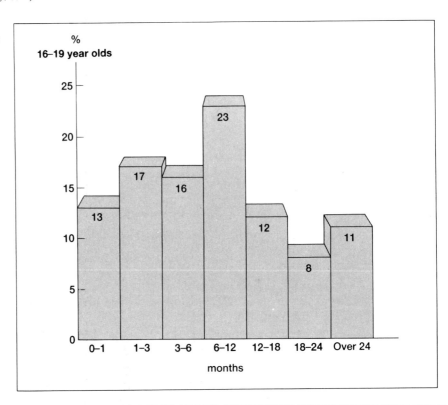

(Source: Labour Force Survey, 1983)

7.2   Satisfaction at work

Work takes up a very large part of our lives. Work can be enjoyable or it can be very boring. It can be a major interest in your life or something that you put up with simply to earn a wage. To some people work is valued because of the money it provides. Yet others get pleasure from the work itself. They enjoy working and their work gives them satisfaction which may be just as important as the money it earns.

When the main reason for working is to earn money which can be spent on other things, the satisfaction is *extrinsic*, or outside of work. Those who enjoy work for itself, who have a job which is itself satisfying, get *intrinsic* satisfaction. Their satisfaction is found in the work.

Work can be enjoyable for many reasons. When you ask people what they like about their job they often point to the people they work with. Being in a group, having a good laugh, working with your mates, are all important at work.

Figure 7.6 Satisfaction at work

(Source: adapted from *Sociology, Work and Industry* by T. J. Watson, Figure 4.1, page 116, RKP, 1980)

Having some control over your work and being able to use your initiative are also important. In many methods of production the workers have little control over the work. The speed of the machine will often control the rate at which someone works. Machines may even control the way the job is done. This gives the worker little chance of personal satisfaction or enjoyment.

Many jobs require skill. People take pride in being able to use their skills to do a good job. Craft workers have always valued their skills and have passed this sense of pride on to apprentices and trainees. This sense of being able to do a good job well is another way in which workers gain satisfaction.

Job satisfaction is not easy to achieve. A good employer knows that satisfied workers are going to work better and produce better products. They do all that they can to provide their workers with the right working conditions and to involve them in making decisions.

When workers are unsatisfied with their work they are said to be alienated. The main causes of *alienation* are a sense of powerlessness, the feeling of having no control over the work; monotony, which is often caused by doing the same thing over and over again; and isolation, being cut off from other people. When workers are alienated they work less well, are more likely to be off sick and to show their dissatisfaction through industrial sabotage or strike action.

CASE STUDY

Making work more satisfying

A factory making electronic parts for television sets was faced with a very high level of absence by the workers. The amount of time that the workers were absent was far more than would have normally been expected in such a factory. The workers in the factory were asked why they thought this was. There were many answers like 'if only I could organise my time the way I want to' and 'if only I could be trained to do some of the other jobs as well'.

Using the worker's comments as a guide, the managers decided to re-organise the way one part of the factory worked. Instead of a row of thirty people, each making one small component, the workers were put into groups of twelve. Each group worked as a team making the whole product. They discussed what needed to be done, the best ways of doing it and then decided who would do what.

The result was that absenteeism fell, productivity and quality increased and the workers felt that they were getting more of a say in the way the work was organised.

A quality circle at Wedgewood's pottery factory discuss ways of improving production.

Discussion

Which of the following situations are examples of:
a intrinsic satisfaction? **b** extrinsic satisfaction?

Figure 7.7 Job satisfaction grid

	Satisfaction at work is:	
	Intrinsic	Extrinsic
a She enjoyed the job at the travel agent's because the work itself was interesting		
b He didn't really like the job but the pay was good and he looked forward to the weekends		
c. The best thing about the job was getting paid at the end of the week		
d He enjoyed the job because of the responsibility it gave him		
e She felt that she had learned a lot by working there and it had made her a better person		
f The job itself was pretty boring but they were a nice group of people to work with		
g The job was great. It was a real challenge		

Figure 7·8

7.3   Work status

Look in the window of the Job Centre or the 'Jobs Vacant' pages of a newspaper. The jobs that are advertised are often very different. They involve using different skills, having different qualifications and kinds of experience and are paid at different rates.

This is all part of the division of labour. Each job is one small part of the total process. The people who work at each job specialise in that particular activity. It is often not easy to move from one job to another because you will not have the right training, skills, qualifications or experience.

It is sometimes possible to 'start at the bottom' and 'work your way up'. The experience gained 'on the job' is then important for promotion. Some jobs require particular qualifications before you can even start on the career ladder. You may need a university degree or even a long period of professional training. Doctors, for example, have to be trained for up to seven years before they qualify.

Different jobs have different rates of pay. They may also have different *fringe benefits*. These could include the use of a company car or just starting work later in the morning without having to 'clock-in'.

Figure 7·9 Fringe benefits

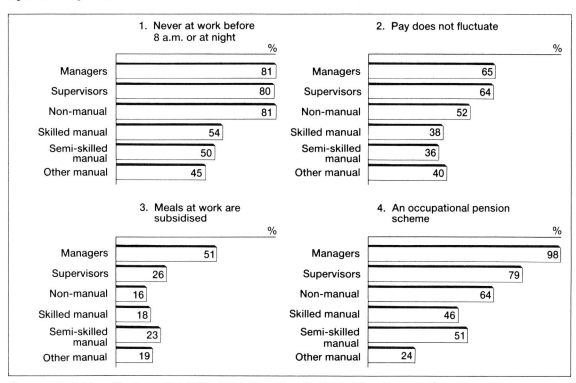

(Source: adapted from *The State of the Nation* by S.Fothergill and J. Vincent, Pluto Press, 1985)

All of these differences add up to different levels of *status* at work. It is not just that people in the top jobs get better pay, they also tend to get better working conditions and fringe benefits. There is often a clear divide between the pay and conditions of the manual workers in the factory and those of the managers in the offices.

Some employers do recognise that these status differences are not only unfair but also inefficient. In these firms everyone from the managing director to the cleaner have to clock-on in the morning and they all eat in the same canteen.

Status and class

Status differences at work are part of the pattern of social class within society. Those who have the better qualifications, have been to the right schools, start off higher up the ladder and end up in the top jobs generally come from the middle classes.

There are men and women from working class backgrounds who do end up in the top jobs. There are people from middle class homes who become manual workers. This movement between classes is known as social mobility. Most people end up in a job which is not very different in status from that of their parents. Most social mobility is a matter of moving up a little or down a little.

Figure 7·10 Social mobility

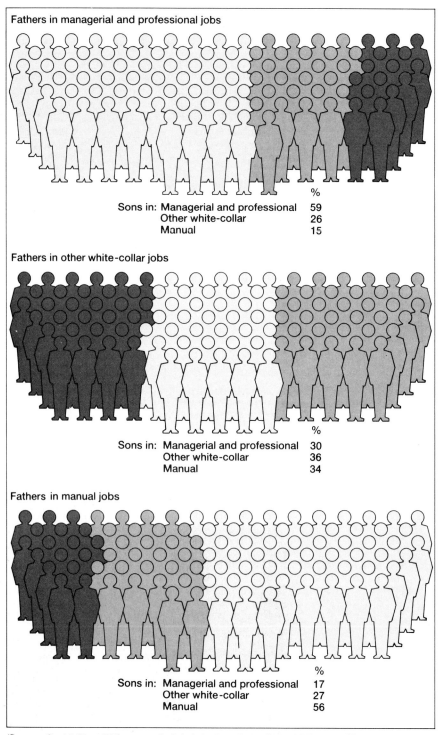

Fathers in managerial and professional jobs

Sons in: Managerial and professional   59
Other white-collar   26
Manual   15

Fathers in other white-collar jobs

Sons in: Managerial and professional   30
Other white-collar   36
Manual   34

Fathers in manual jobs

Sons in: Managerial and professional   17
Other white-collar   27
Manual   56

(Source: *Social Class Differences in Britain* by Ivan Reid, Grant McIntyre, 1981)

7.4 Working women

Two out of every five workers in Britain are women.

The working lives of women are very different from those of men. Women are more likely to work part-time. They do different types of work and are less likely to get the top jobs. They are generally less well paid. Their careers are often interrupted when they have children.

Women are often seen first as housewives and mothers and only secondly as workers in offices, schools and factories. It is often thought that women go out to work for the 'extras' and that their wages are not as important as men's. Most families with working mothers, however, could not survive without the money that they earn. There are many single women who support themselves.

Two out of every five women who work full-time are employed in clerical and secretarial work. Three-quarters of all full-time clerical workers are women. Only one in every twenty managers is a woman.

Certain jobs are seen as 'woman's work'. This includes work in hospitals and schools as well as making clothes and selling. Often these are jobs which require less skill.

A civil engineer working on a new airport.

Figure 7·11 Women in the labour market

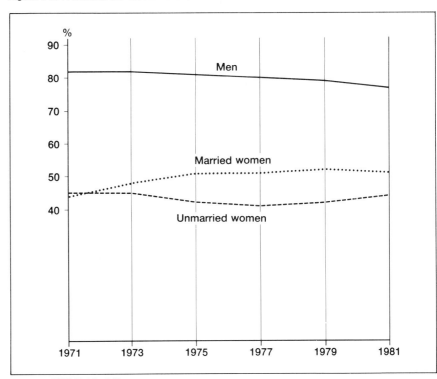

(Source: GHS, Table 4·1)

Discrimination

Women are discriminated against at work in many ways. Their pay is lower, they have less opportunity to undertake training or to share in fringe benefits such as pension schemes. Women are more likely to do part-time work. Part-time workers do not have the same advantages as full-time workers.

Parliament has passed laws which are intended to prevent discrimination against women. These are the Equal Pay Act 1970 and the Sex Discrimination Act 1975. Men and women are to be paid the same for the same work. It is unlawful for an employer to discriminate directly (such as by rules which only allow men to apply to certain jobs) or indirectly, by making it difficult for women to apply for certain jobs. These laws have helped women to improve their position but have not given women full equality.

Housework

Housework is unpaid domestic labour. Traditionally it is seen as 'a woman's job'. Although men help with household jobs they don't always help with everything.

Housework has its good and bad points. Many women find it monotonous and repetitive. There is a constant pressure to get it done. It is a job that never ends. As soon as the house is clean it is time to start cleaning it all over again. On the other hand the independence that goes with housework is often important. Many housewives like to be able to plan their own day and to organise the work for themselves. They are their own bosses.

Housework has to be done even when women work full-time. Women often have two roles. They are housewives and wage-earners.

Table 7.3   Women at work, 1982

	Women	Men	Women's earnings/hours as % of men's
Average weekly earnings	£99	£154.5	64%
Average weekly hours	37.1	41.7	89%
Average hourly earnings	£2.67	£3.70	72%

(Source: *New Earnings Survey 1982*, in *Your Rights at Work* by J. McMullen, Pluto Press, 1983, Table 3)

Table 7.4   How often does your husband help by changing the baby's dirty nappy?

Social class	Never, seldom, or only under protest %	Usually %
Working class	85	15
Middle class	65	35

(Source: *Sociology of Housework* by A. Oakley, Martin Robertson, 1974, Table 8.6)

Questions
1. Which group of workers – men, married women or unmarried women – is more likely to be working in 1981 than in 1971?
2. Has the Equal Pay Act give women equal pay with men?
3. What reasons are there for the differences between the earnings of men and women?
4. How does social class influence the way men help in the home?
5. In which industries are women most likely to be employed?

7.5   Trade unions

Two hundred years ago working people had little protection against unemployment, illness or low wages. In order to provide for themselves they began to organise Friendly Societies. A few pennies were paid each week and in return the worker and his family received help if they were sick or unemployed. At this time it was illegal for workers to join together to improve their pay or working conditions. It was not until the middle of the nineteenth century that the beginnings of our modern trade unions began to appear.

Right from the start, unions had to struggle to gain the right to take action on behalf of their members. Employers used the courts to control the power of the unions. Gradually the unions, working through the Labour Party in Parliament, changed the law and established their rights. The unions' struggle for their members' rights still continues today.

The early unions represented the interests of different groups of workers. The *craft unions* were made up of skilled workers in particular trades. *Industrial unions* included workers who did many different jobs but in the same industry. A third group of unions included workers in

Figure 7·12 Trade union membership 1951–1981 (millions)

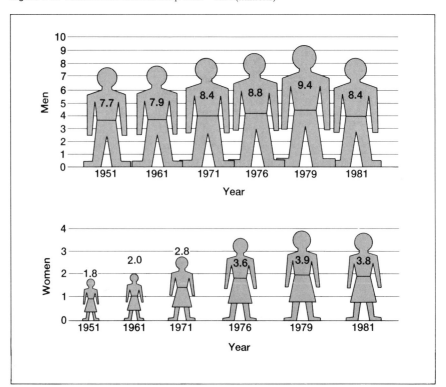

(Source: *Social Trends*, 1985, Table 11·10)

different jobs who worked in different industries. These *general unions* often included the lowest paid workers. *White-collar unions* for teachers, nurses, bank employees and local government workers have grown rapidly in the last thirty years.

The membership of trade unions was highest at the end of the 1970s. Since then the total membership of trade unions has fallen. This fall in membership has been greatest in the declining industries. Where there are fewer workers there are fewer people to join unions. These changes have affected unions in different ways.

Some unions have joined forces to create larger, general unions. Many of the smaller unions have disappeared. Disputes within some unions and disagreements over union policy have, in some cases, led to breakaway unions being established. It has been the unions of white-collar workers and the lower paid which have seen an increase in their membership.

Figure 7·13 Changes in union membership 1979–82

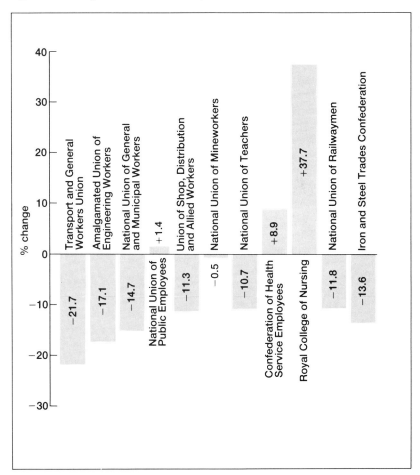

(Source: *Social Trends*, 1985, Table 11·11)

The role of the unions

Unions work for their members in many ways. As well as looking after their members' interests at work, negotiating pay and working conditions, the union will also provide help for members who are unable to work through sickness. Union social funds support the widows and children of members who have died and provide homes for retired union members. The unions also provide legal help and advice for members on such matters as unfair dismissal, redundancy and equal pay.

Trade unions come together in the Trades Union Congress. The TUC has little direct power over individual unions but provides a basis for the unions to share and discuss common problems. It also provides an organisation that can meet and discuss important issues at a national level with employers' associations, such as the Confederation of British Industry, and with the government.

Trade unions and the law

Both Labour and Conservative governments have passed laws to control the activities of trade unions. These laws have aimed to protect the rights of individuals, to strengthen union democracy and to reduce the effect of strikes.

Closed shop agreements mean that all workers in a particular factory or firm must belong to a recognised union. This has often been considered unfair by workers who do not wish to belong to any union, or who wish to join a union that has not been recognised. The unions, and many employers, support 'the closed shop' because it makes its negotiations over pay and conditions simpler.

Sometimes disputes cannot be settled by negotiation and lead to strikes. Before a strike can be called there must be a ballot of the union members. When they go on strike the workers 'picket' the factory gate to try to persuade other workers not to work. This is perfectly legal. Secondary picketing, where workers picket other firms not connected with the dispute in order to bring more pressure to bear on the employer, is not allowed by the law.

The trade unions are an important source of money for the Labour Party, in the same way that the Conservatives depend upon donations from businesses. Before a union can use its political funds in this way it must ballot its members. This is also intended to protect the rights of individual union members.

The TUC conference meeting at Brighton in 1984.

Questions
1. What are the different types of unions? Which groups of workers do they represent?
2. Trade unions are not only concerned with striking for better wages. What else do they do for their members?
3. In what ways are unions democratic?
4. What are the national bodies which:
   a represent the interests of the trade unions?
   b represent the interests of employers?
5. What is meant by:
   a the closed shop?   **c** negotiation?
   b secondary picketing?   **d** political funds?

7.6 Leisure

There are many ways of using your leisure-time. Sometimes the things that people do in their leisure-time look very much like work. It is not always easy to decide where work ends and leisure begins. Imagine a football match on a Saturday afternoon. To the spectators it is probably part of their leisure. Television commentators watch the same game but to them it is work. The commentators are paid to be at the game and have no choice in the matter. The spectators, on the other hand, are there because they want to be.

This example shows a number of the differences between leisure and work. People are usually paid to work whereas they are not paid for leisure. In your leisure you do what you want to, whereas at work you usually have to do what other people want you to do. For most people work and leisure happen at different times and in different places.

Holiday-makers on the beach at Scarborough in 1913.

Changes in leisure

People have not always had a great deal of leisure. During the Industrial Revolution, factory workers spent their days off cleaning the machines. Employers thought that the workers would grow idle if they were allowed any free time.

Towards the end of the nineteenth century it was realised that giving workers time to relax and 're-charge their batteries' helped them to work better. At about the same time the railways made day-trips to the sea-side easier and cheaper. The trade unions campaigned for a shorter working week and holidays with pay.

It was not enough to give workers more leisure time if they could not afford to do things in it. As wages rose people began to have spare money that could be used for leisure activities. At first they would have spent it on a 'wireless set', a bicycle or a visit to the cinema. Later this became a colour television and holidays in Spain. As more and more money was spent on leisure it began to develop as an important industry.

Figure 7·14 An average week

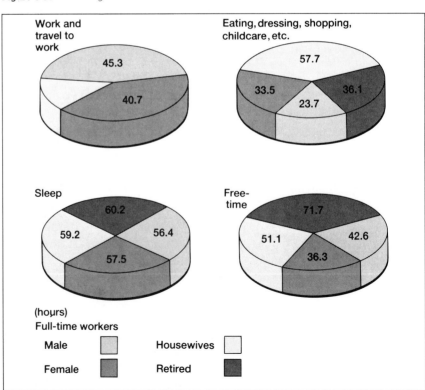

Figure 7·15 Men and women in different kinds
of job were asked if they have been
involved in certain activities in the previous four weeks

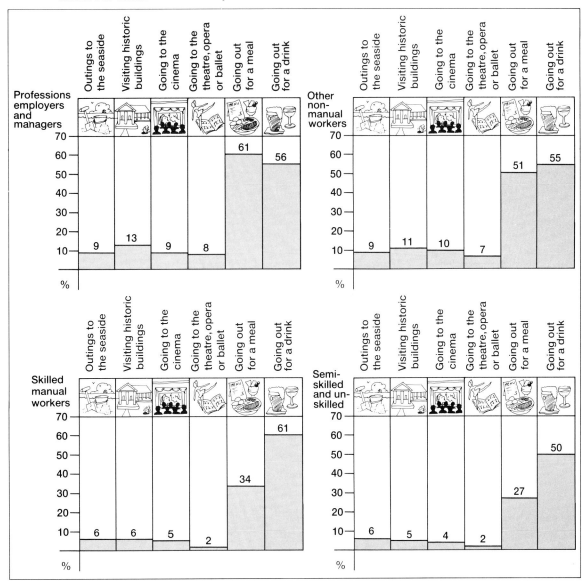

Leisure patterns

Different groups in society use their leisure time in different ways. This
is partly because they choose to do different things but also because
some groups can afford to spend more on their leisure. If you have a
car, for example, it is easier to get out and do more. Middle class families
are more likely to go on outings to the seaside or into the country.

On the whole men and women use their leisure in similar ways except
that men are more likely to be working around the house and on DIY

while women are more likely to spend time knitting. There are also class differences in the choice of leisure activity. Fewer manual workers go out for a meal. They are more likely to go out to the pub.

The actual job that you do may also influence how you spend your leisure. For some people leisure and work are not very different. What they do in their own time is an extension of what they do at work. An engineer who repairs old steam trains at the weekend; a doctor who helps with St John's Ambulance or Red Cross are examples of how work extends into leisure.

Other people see leisure as the complete opposite of work. The things that they do at weekends are as far away as possible from what they do in the week. Leisure provides an opportunity to do something different. Between these two extremes there are many people whose leisure is probably different from their work but they don't think of it that way. The connection is fairly neutral.

Project

Figure 7.15 shows some of the ways in which people spend their leisure time. It does not show how leisure is used by different age groups. Nor does it include leisure activities like watching football, going to discos or fishing.

Conduct a survey to find out how different age groups use their leisure time.

An important influence on HOW people use their leisure time is WHAT facilities are available to them. After all, you cannot go windsurfing if there are no watersports areas, or practice skiing if there is no dry ski-slope. Use your survey to find out WHAT leisure facilities people really want.

7.7   Vocabulary

Alienation

Alienation simply means 'becoming separated'. It can be used to describe how someone feels about something or someone and is also used when workers are 'separated' in some way from the results of their work.

Assembly line

A method of production in which the product moves from one stage of manufacture to another on a track or conveyor belt.

Automation

The use of computerised machines which are able to manufacture articles without supervision and which can often make simple decisions.

Batch production

A method of production which makes products in 'batches' of similar articles before being re-organised to produce a batch of another article.

Closed shop

In a closed shop all of the workers must belong to a trade union.

Confederation of British Industry (CBI)	The organisation which represents employers and their organisations.
Craft union	A trade union whose members all work in the same trade, or craft, though often in different industries.
Extrinsic satisfaction	Satisfaction that is gained outside of the work.
General union	A union whose members work at many different trades in a number of different industries.
Industrial union	A trade union whose members all work in the same industry though often at different jobs.
Intrinsic satisfaction	Satisfaction that is gained from work itself.
Instrumental approach to work	Working only for what you can get out of work with no satisfaction from the work itself.
Picketing	Attempting to persuade other workers not to go into work during a strike.
Secondary picketing	Picketing that takes place at a place of work not directly involved in a strike.
Trades Union Congress	The national organisation made up of all of the main trade unions and which represents their views.
White-collar union	A trade union whose members are employed in office or technical jobs.

CHAPTER 8

BUYING AND SELLING

What would life be like without money?

How would you buy anything, or pay for an evening out? What would you use to save for a holiday or for Christmas? How would you know what anything was worth?

Only the very simplest societies can operate without money in some form. When there is no money people trade by exchanging goods. This method of exchange is known as *barter*. A cheese will be bartered for eggs, a goat, for so many lambs. Craftsmen will be paid in corn or meat. Payment in goods instead of money is called 'payment in kind'.

Barter is a very inefficient way of trading. Before trade can begin there must be buyers and sellers who want what each other has. Buyers and sellers must haggle over the value of everything. If goods are kept for too long they begin to perish and lose their value. It is very difficult to save for the future.

Money makes trading much simpler. Instead of exchanging cheese for eggs, or sheep for corn, the farmer can get money for them. This money can either be saved or used to buy other things that are needed.

Not all money is made up of coins or paper notes. Money needn't be at all like the money that we know. Seashells, animal teeth, skins and pebbles are used as money. In prison, cigarettes are a form of money. School pupils trade with conkers. Anything which is generally accepted in payment of a debt can be thought of as money.

8.1   Money

Money has a number of uses. When you go shopping you use money as a *medium of exchange*. Coins and notes are exchanged for the goods in the shop. By using money you also know what the goods you are buying will cost. Money is used as a *unit of account*.

Money also enables you to look ahead to things you might buy in the future. If you want a loan to buy a new stereo, money makes it possible to calculate your repayments. Imagine what it would be like to repay a loan with one chicken and three dozen eggs each week for a year. Money is a way of repaying debts.

You may not want to spend your money. You may wish to save it. Whether you put it in a bank or under the floorboards the money will still be there when you want it (so long as it hasn't been stolen!). It will not have perished or decayed. In this way money is a *store of value*.

As well as being accepted payment for goods and services money also needs to be fairly rare. There is no point in having money which is freely available. If money really did 'grow on trees' no one would use it because it would have no value. This is why certain rare metals, such as silver and gold, have often been used.

Gold coins are valuable for the metal that they contain. Money may also have a value because of what it represents. A one-pound coin contains much less than one-pound's worth of metal and certainly costs much less than one pound to produce. It is worth one pound because people will take it in payment for things that are valued at one pound. It is *token* money which only has a value in exchange.

Figure 8·1

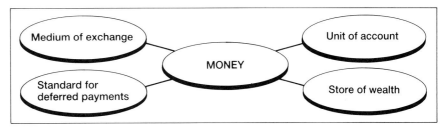

Other forms of money

In a modern economy the total supply of money is far more than just cash, in the form of notes and coins, that is in everyday use. Cash is only one of the types of money that can be used in buying and selling. Watch people doing their shopping. They often buy things without ever using any cash. They pay by cheque or use credit cards. They may even have accounts with the store in which they shop or use luncheon vouchers in a restaurant.

A cheque by itself is not money. It has no value other than the paper on which it is printed. A cheque is simply an instruction to a bank to

Electronic banking is a feature of every High Street.

transfer some money from one bank account to another. The money that the cheque represents is in the bank account.

Instead of using cash or cheques some people use plastic cards as money. Cheque cards are a form of identity card used when paying by cheque. Cashcards carry information which can be read by computers. These can be used at any time of day or night in cash machines outside banks and building societies. Credit cards and charge cards can be used to pay for goods in shops, for hotel bills, mail order and even telephone calls. At the end of the month the card-holder is sent details of what has been spent, and may either pay it all or have credit to an agreed amount.

In the future, electronic banking will mean that there will be even less need for cash. Shops will be equipped to read information from the cards and to transfer the required amount directly from the customer's bank account. No cash will change hands and there will be no need for cheques.

Discussion

If money is going to be useful it needs to be convenient and easy to use. It should be hard-wearing but not too heavy to carry around. There should be large denominations for expensive purchases but these should be broken down into smaller units for small payments.

Which of the following items would make good money?

Figure 8.2

	Valued for itself	Easy to carry around	Hard-wearing	Easy to divide	In limited supply
Wooden beads					
Gold coins					
Sunflower seeds					
Cigarettes					
Cucumbers					
Shells					
Credit cards					
Round pebbles					
Printed paper					

At one time the Bank of England issued coins worth $\frac{1}{2}$p and notes for £1. The old ten shillings note was replaced by the 50p coin and £2 coins were introduced. Why do you think these changes were made?

8.2 Money, banking and insurance

The banks look after money that has been deposited with them by their customers. When the bank's customers want to pay for something they write a cheque. This tells the bank to pay out some of the money that has been deposited. These payments are often to people who also have bank accounts. The payment simply means making a change in the bank's books. Only a very small part of the money is ever needed as cash. The banks are able to lend out most of the money that has been deposited. Those who borrow money from the bank pay interest.

Most of the High Street banks are branches of one of the 'big four' banks: Lloyds, Midland, Barclay's and National Westminster. There are also a number of smaller banks including the Scottish Banks, the Co-operative Bank and the Trustee Savings Bank. These banks provide services for the ordinary customer as well as to businesses.

In the City of London there are *merchant banks* which provide specialist banking services for large companies and for the financial markets. At the centre of the banking system is the Bank of England which is different from all of the other banks. It is the government's bank. It is also where the other banks keep some of their money. Through its influence over interest rates and government borrowing it is able to control the whole banking system. In England it is the only bank that has the right to print banknotes.

The modern banking system does more than just look after people's money. It makes it possible for millions of people to pay their bills and

Figure 8·3 The clearing system

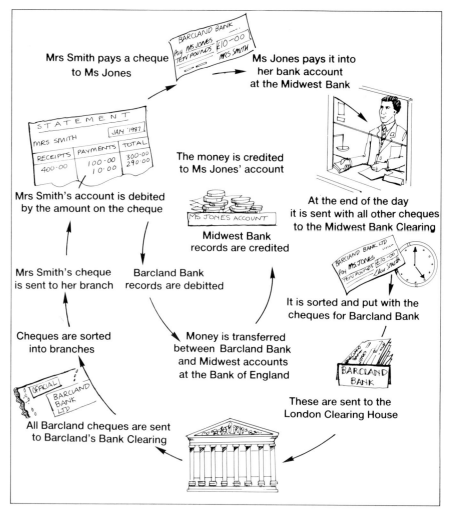

do their shopping without having to carry around large amounts of cash. Even so, on an average day 600 payments are made every second, and 94% of these are in cash. Most of these payments are fairly small, often less than one pound. For larger payments many people prefer to use cheques.

Everyday millions of cheques pass through the banking system. These may be for as little as a few pounds for someone's electricity bill or as much as millions of pounds for a large business transaction. A cheque may be paid into any one of the thousands of bank branches across the country. It will end up in the branch where the account is held and the money is paid. This massive movement of cheques is carried out through the Bank Clearing System.

Many people have their wages paid by cheque, or straight into their bank account. They can pay bills by cheque or take out cash, either over the counter at the bank or through an automatic cash dispenser. Regular bills can be paid through standing orders or direct debits. Banks also provide loans, foreign currency for when you travel abroad, deposit accounts for your savings and advice on investments as well as many other services.

Insurance

Insurance protects you against risks. Any risk which could cause you to lose money can be insured against. You can insure your house against fire or burglary and your car against accidents. Firms insure against claims from customers and losses while goods are in transit.

The insurance companies know from experience the likelihood of any event taking place. In other words, they know what the risks are. They also know what it will cost to make good any loss that might result from that event. They can then spread the likely cost around all of those who face that risk. Everyone has the benefit of the insurance protection and some also receive the compensation.

Many things can be insured. Your life can be insured to provide money for your dependents. Your belongings can be insured against theft. A dancer's legs or a musicians hands can be insured. Wherever there is a financial risk there can be insurance. The person who takes out the insurance must have an 'insurable interest'. You could not, for example, insure someone else's house. It must also be a risk that can be calculcated.

Discussion

Which of the following risks could be insured against?

Figure 8.4

	You can only insure against financial loss	Losses must be accidental	The insurer must be able to calculate the risk	There must be many similar risks
Losing a bet on a horse-race				
Losing all of your money on holiday				
Having your camera stolen				
Being jilted by your boy/girl friend				

8.3   The Kapauku of Papua New Guinea

Figure 8·5

New Guinea

Australia

0   1000 km

The Kapauku live in the mountain forests of Papua New Guinea. The land they inhabit is many days' journey from the sea. The steep mountain valleys mean that the Kapauku have little contact with other tribes.

The forest is not rich in animals and the people could not survive by hunting. Instead they are farmers. Their most important crop is the yam or sweet potato which is food for pigs as well as people. The pigs are an important part of the Kapaukun economy. They are more than a valuable source of food. Pigs are important for the great ceremonies when many pigs are roasted on large fires. Breeding and selling pigs provides the farmer both with money and with status.

To gain wealth and status a young man must become a farmer. He must buy land and the sweet potatoes to plant on it. When the potato vines have grown he must buy a pig. To do this he must borrow money from his relatives. In time the pig will produce young. The male piglets will be sold and the sows used for breeding. More land will be needed to provide sweet potatoes to feed the growing herd of pigs. He will need help to weed the gardens of sweet potato and will buy a wife.

Shell money

Even in such a small-scale society the economy depends upon buying and selling; none of which would be possible without some form of money.

For the Kapauku money means cowrie shells and shell-necklaces. The shells come from the coast. The journey is difficult and the shells are not easy to obtain. They are usually acquired in trade with people from other tribes.

As with most forms of money the cowrie shells come in different sizes or denominations. The smallest are called *kawane*. The larger *bomoje* shells are worth between fifteen and twenty kawane. The necklaces, of smaller shells or glass beads and as long as a man's arm, are worth one bomoje.

Fixing a price

Most of the things that a man would want to buy have a customary price. A piece of land will cost 5 bomoje shells, two kilos of pork costs 1 bomoje and a whole pig 20 bomoje. The customary price may sometimes change. A sale to a relative will usually be at a cheaper price. When pigs are scarce the price will rise, often to three times the customary price.

The sale of pigs can take place at any time. Most of the trading, however, takes place at special ceremonies when as many as a thousand buyers and sellers gather to trade and to settle their debts. At these markets hundreds of pigs will change hands.

Amongst the Kapauku there is a price for everything. Shells must be paid as a bride price at a wedding, or to compensate for grief at a funeral. Shells may also be invested. A man will lend shells to his relative and expect them to be returned with a little extra added to them. A wealthy man may even collect rare shells, and hide them away until the price has risen. He will then sell them at a profit.

Although their money is different the Kapauku buy and sell in much the same way as people elsewhere in the world.

Shell money

Questions
1. Why do shells make a good form of money for the Kapauku?
2. How do the Kapauku fix the prices of the things they buy and sell?
3. When does most of the trade in pigs take place?
4. How might shell-money be used as an investment?

8.4   Buying and selling

Markets

Most towns have a market on one or two days during the week. There
are outdoor markets with many different stalls under brightly coloured
canopies and more permanent indoor markets. In country towns the
market stalls are only one part of a bigger, and more important, market
to which farmers bring their animals for sale.

The trading floor of the
London Metal Exchange

There are other markets which look very different from the sort of
places where you go to buy clothes and vegetables. In the City of London
there are *commodity markets* where dealers trade in copper and zinc,
cocoa and coffee beans. In these markets there is no sign of the goods
that are being bought and sold. The dealers may never actually see
what they are buying. There are also financial markets such as the Stock
Exchange.

Any group of buyers and sellers who agree a price for a particular
product make up a market. This may involve two people haggling over
the price to be paid for a used car, three hundred people making bids
for a work-of-art in a public auction, or dealers in London, Tokyo and
New York agreeing prices they will pay for dollars and francs.

A market does not even need to exist in a particular place. The market
in foreign currencies is a truly global market. Buyers and sellers in
capital cities throughout the world are linked by telephone lines and
computer networks.

Figure 8·6 The foreign exchange market

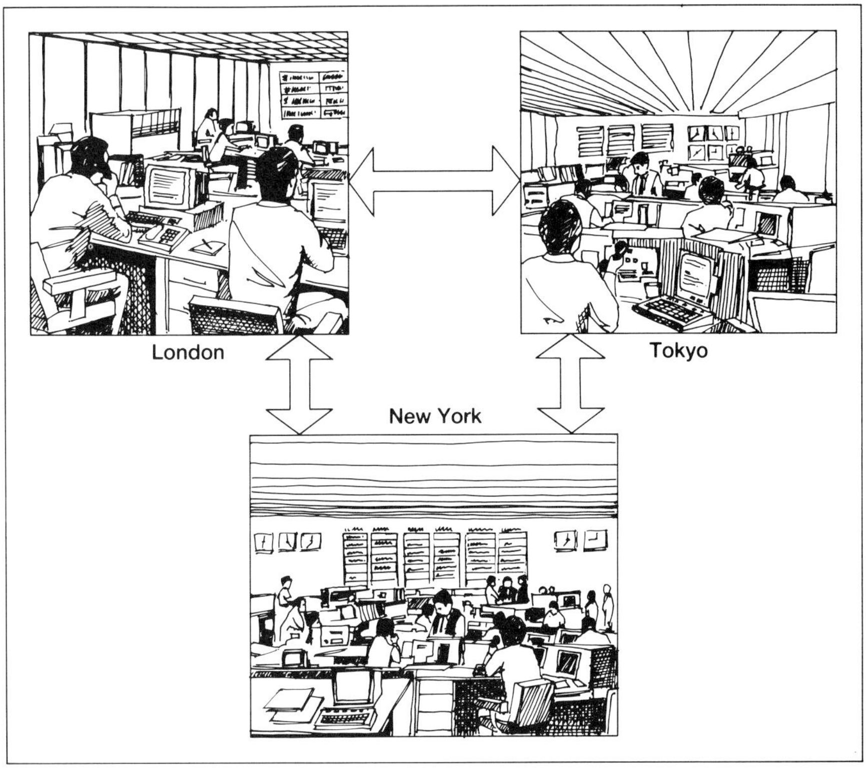

The retailer

For most people contact with the market-place is in the High Street or the local shopping centre. They may do their shopping at the corner shop, in a store in the city centre, through a mail-order catalogue or from a door-to-door salesman. These are all different types of retailer.

Retailing has changed considerably in the past few years. The smaller family-run shops have gradually disappeared. In their place are branches of large retailing chains, or multiples. Some of these are specialist chain stores which trade in a particular range of goods, such as food, clothes or electrical products. Others sell a wide variety of products.

The chain stores have many advantages over the small independent retailer. They can often deal directly with the manufacturers, cutting out the wholesalers who supply the smaller shops. The amount they sell enables them to buy in bulk, often at a cheaper price. They may even market some products of their own under a 'brand name'.

The independent retailer, on the other hand, can often provide services that would not be economic for a multiple store. Independent corner shops are sited away from the main shopping centres. They can

provide a more personal service, often stocking a wider range of goods. The smaller shops can often cater for a more specialist market, drawing on a wider area through mail order selling.

Large stores need to be able to sell a very large number of goods if they are to make a profit. It is important to have a high turnover. This means that the retailer must deal with very large numbers of customers and have space to store all that they might need. A shop site in the local High Street will not only be expensive to rent but may also be limited in space. Without extensive car parking such shops will often be difficult to get to. A large retailer may find it more profitable to build a new store on a 'green field' site at the edge of town or in an area which is being re-developed. These stores, often looking more like warehouses than shops, serve a much wider area. They depend upon shoppers being able to drive to them and to park their cars while they shop. They are known as hypermarkets.

Project

Carry out a survey into the shopping habits of the families of the people in your class.

1. Where do people shop?
2. Which kinds of retailer do people use, and what for?
3. How often do they use particular types of retailer?
4. Why do they shop in particular places?

8.5   Price

How does a manufacturer decide what price to charge?

Firstly there will be the costs of production. There will then be distribution costs in getting the product to the customer, and the cost of advertising the product. Wholesalers and retailers will add their expenses and profits to the final cost of the product. If the costs of production and distribution are more than the customers would be prepared to pay then there would be no reason to produce the goods. Some things, however, are sold for far more than they cost to make. Works-of-art do not cost a great deal to produce yet they are often sold for thousands of pounds.

For every product on the market there are a number of people who are prepared to buy it at a certain price. We can call this the *demand* for the product. At a certain price manufacturers are prepared to produce a certain number of goods. This is the *supply*.

As the price of the product falls more people will be prepared to buy it, but, at the same time, manufacturers will produce less. They will prefer to direct their energies towards making goods which will sell more easily, or at a higher price. When prices rise the opposite happens. People will buy less while producers will want to produce more.

Selling pocket televisions

An electronics firm have developed a new pocket television. Market research has given them details of the number of televisions that are likely to be demanded by the public at different prices. They can plot these figures on a demand graph.

Figure 8·7 The demand for pocket television sets

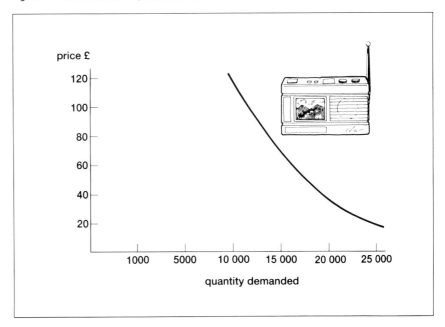

The firm's accountants have calculated how many they can afford to produce at each price if they are to make a reasonable profit. These figures go on to a supply graph.

If the two graphs are put together the lines for supply and demand cross. At this price the number of pocket televisions that they are prepared to supply is the same as the number that people will be prepared to buy. At this price, supply and demand are said to be in equilibrium. The firm will make 17 000 televisions to sell at £50.

Supply and demand for different products are often linked. If you produce more beef you must also produce more hides for leather. If demand for beef rises and more is produced there could be a fall in the price of leather because more is now being supplied.

Some products are demanded together. When the price of strawberries is low and more people are buying them the demand for cream will probably be high. Other goods are alternatives. You would

probably eat butter or margarine, but not both. In the same way some
goods are produced alternatively. Milk can be used either to drink, to

Figure 8·8 The supply of pocket television sets

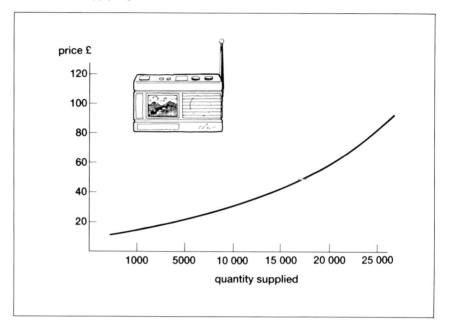

Figure 8·9 Supply and demand for pocket television sets

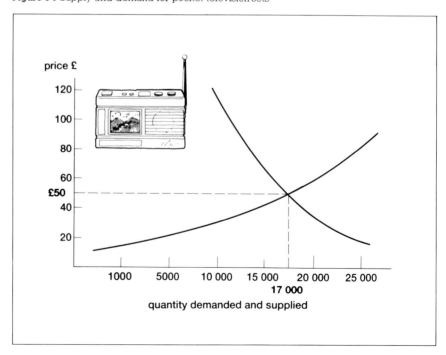

make butter or to make cheese. If more milk is used for cheese, less will be available for butter.

The ways in which supply and demand for different goods are linked has an effect on prices.

Value

All commodities are scarce. There are never enough to go around. The money that people have is limited. Because we cannot have everything that we might want we have to make choices.

People will only buy things if they believe that they are worth the money. Goods and services have a value to those who might wish to buy them. If the price is greater than the value that people place on the goods then they will choose not to buy.

The value that anyone gives to something depends upon how they want it. This will depend upon how much use the item is to them. A rowing boat is not much use to someone in the middle of a desert or on top of a mountain. It is quite useful at the seaside. Economists describe the usefulness of things to different people as the *utility* of the goods.

In real life the more that we have of something the less we are likely to want more of it, and therefore the less value we place on each extra item. It is the usefulness of each extra purchase that helps us decide when we do not wish to buy any more. This is the *marginal utility* of the goods we are buying.

The value placed on something also depends on what we must do without if we buy it. Because our money is always limited buying one thing means doing without something else. Each time we buy something we lose the opportunity to spend money on other things. This is the *opportunity cost* of making the purchase.

Discussion

The government has placed a tax on records. This tax doubles the cost of record albums but does not affect other forms of recorded music. What will be the effect on:

a the demand for record albums?
b the price of raw vinyl (used to make records)?
c the price of compact disc players?
d the demand for recorded cassettes?

8.6   Inflation

Money is a commodity. It can be bought and sold like any other commodity. This means that it has a price and is affected by supply and demand. Coins and notes have a face value stamped or printed on them and a real value which is what it is worth in exchange. When prices rise in the shops the real value of money falls. This happens during periods of *inflation*.

If there is too much money in circulation people will place less value on it. This means that they will want more of it in exchange for goods. Prices will then rise.

Inflation happens when there is too much money chasing too few goods. We know it is happening when we see prices rising in the shops. A rise in prices is the same as a fall in the value of money. In a period of inflation money is worth less.

There is nothing new about inflation. In the sixteenth century Spanish explorers in South America discovered large amounts of gold and silver. This vast treasure was brought back to Europe where it gradually became part of the money supply. This sudden increase in the amount of money in Europe led to massive inflation as all of the extra money created an increased demand for goods.

Governments can make more money just by printing it. After the First World War the German government tried to pay its debts by printing more money. This caused the value of the German mark to fall. Prices more than doubled every month. By 1923 workers were having to collect their wages in suitcases and a loaf of bread cost over 400 billion marks. Inflation at such a rate is known as hyperinflation.

In the early 1920s the German currency suffered from massive inflation. This shopkeeper had to keep the notes in the tea-chest as there was no room for them in the till.

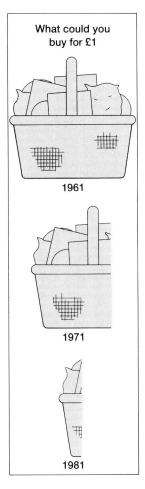

Figure 8·10 Purchasing power

What could you buy for £1

1961

1971

1981

The causes of inflation

Inflation is not always as spectacular as that in Germany in the 1920s. Prices can be *pushed up* by increasing costs of production or *pulled-up* by greater demand.

If wages or the cost of raw materials rise, it will lead to higher prices. The sudden rise in the price of oil from the Middle East in 1974 caused an increase in the costs of industrial production and set off a period of rising inflation. Sometimes wages rise more than the output of the factories. This also can lead to higher inflation. Some economists and politicians argue that trade unions have gained too much power to force employers to pay high wages and that this forces up prices.

The government may borrow in order to pay for public spending. If the government allows public spending to rise too fast and has to borrow too much then the result might be more inflation.

Finally, inflation may be caused by an increase in the amount of bank lending. Bank deposits are a form of money. If too much is lent out for people to spend then that has the same effect as increasing the money supply by printing more.

The control of inflation

Most countries have some inflation. The control of inflation has been an important political issue in recent years. Keeping inflation under control is not always easy.

Wage increases may be kept low and bank lending can be controlled. This can be done by raising interest rates. This is not always a good idea. Although it keeps bank lending down it also pushes up the cost of borrowing by industry and increases costs of production. Higher bank interest rates also effect the building societies. This leads to more expensive mortgages and more inflation.

Table 8.1   The percentage that average prices increased in each year (rates of inflation)

	1972 1973 %	1973 1974 %	1974 1975 %	1975 1976 %	1976 1977 %	1977 1978 %	1978 1979 %	1979 1980 %	1980 1981 %	1981 1982 %	1982 1983 %
United Kingdom	9.2	16.1	24.2	16.5	15.8	8.3	13.4	18.0	11.9	8.6	4.6
West Germany	6.9	7.0	6.0	4.5	3.7	2.7	4.1	5.5	6.3	5.3	3.3
France	7.3	13.7	11.8	9.6	9.4	9.1	10.8	13.6	13.4	11.8	9.6
Japan	11.7	24.5	11.8	9.3	8.1	3.8	3.6	8.0	4.9	2.7	1.9
USA	6.2	11.0	9.1	5.8	6.5	7.7	11.3	13.5	10.4	6.1	3.2

(Source: *Social Trends*, 1985, Table 6.5, HMSO)

Questions

Table 8.1 shows the rate at which inflation increased in five of the world's major industrial nations between 1973 and 1983.

1. In which country did inflation increase fastest between 1973 and 1974?
2. Which country had the lowest growth in inflation in the ten-year period?
3. Describe the trend in inflation in the United Kingdom between 1973 and 1978.
4. Which country had the greatest increase in inflation between 1982 and 1983?
5. In which country was the growth in inflation lowest between 1978 and 1983?

8.7   The cost of living

No two people spend their money in exactly the same way. Their 'costs-of-living' will be different. If we are to get a picture of the *cost of living* over the whole country we must discover how the 'average' person spends his or her money. We need to know what an 'average' shopping basket would look like.

Once we know this we can find out how much it would cost to buy all of the things in the 'basket'. If we do this regularly we can build a picture of how the cost of the 'average shopping basket' changes. When we do this we must remember that there is no such thing as 'an average person'. The best we can do is to get an idea of how a fairly typical group of people would spend their money.

Keeping track of the cost of this 'average shopping basket' would work quite well over a short period of time. Over a longer period the way our 'average' person spends his or her money is going to change. There will be changes in taste and fashion, new products will come on to the market and life-styles will change. This makes comparisons over longer periods of time more difficult.

To get over this problem we would need to change the contents of our 'shopping basket' regularly. This means that we need regular information about how people spend their money. This information is collected through two enquiries. These are the Family Expenditure Survey (or FES), and the General Index of Retail Prices.

Family Expenditure Survey

Surveys of how people spent their money began as long ago as 1914.
It was not until 1957 that it was decided to set up a regular sample survey
of family expenditure.

The FES is a survey which uses a *multi-stage* method of sampling.
In the first stage the country is divided up into areas and a number
of areas are sampled. In the second stage, 16 addresses are chosen
at random from the electoral registers in each of the areas that have
been chosen. This produces about 10 000 addresses. Seventy percent
of these are usually used in the survey. Addresses may not be used
because people have moved away, or do not wish to co-operate.

The survey is based on households and includes everyone in the
family over the age of sixteen. Information on their income and recent
spending is collected on questionnaires. Everyone is asked to keep a
diary of their spending for two weeks.

The Index of Retail Prices

One of the most important ways in which FES data is used is the General
Index of Retail Prices, or RPI. Using the RPI we can compare prices
now with prices in previous years. There is usually a *base-line* at some
point in the past. The cost-of-living index at that time is taken to be 100.
If prices rise by 10% then the new index will be 110. On a Tuesday,
near the middle of each month, civil servants from over 200 local
employment offices go out and collect the prices of over 300 different
items from local shops. Other prices, such as mortgage interest rates
and postage stamps are collected centrally. The prices used are the
actual prices that are being charged, including offers and genuine
reductions. Each month over 150 000 prices are collected.

The prices are checked and then combined to give an average price
for each item. The information from FES is used to make up the 'shopping
basket' which is used to collect the information for RPI.

Checking prices for the
Retail Prices Index.

Weighting

It is not enough just to know what people buy and what it costs. To get an accurate picture of the cost-of-living we also need to know how important each item is within the whole 'basket' of purchases. This is known as the *weighting*.

If, for some reason, the price of bread went up by one-tenth, it would not lead to a 10% rise in the cost-of-living. In 1985 bread took 1% of the cost of the total 'basket'. This means that it had a 'weighting' of 1% or 10 per thousand. If nothing else changed a 10% rise in the price of a loaf would only lead to a rise of one-tenth of 1% in the total cost-of-living.

The Retail Prices Index is an important source of information for everyone. It helps the government to keep a watch on inflation. Trade unions and employers use it when they negotiate pay rises. Pensions, welfare benefits and savings are often 'index-linked', increasing in value when the Index of Retail Prices goes up.

Table 8.2   Retail Price Index
Weightings, 1985

Food	190
Alcoholic drink	75
Tobacco	37
Housing	153
Fuel and light	65
Household goods	65
Clothing and footwear	75
Transport and vehicles	156
Other goods	77
Services	62
Meals outside the home	45
Total	1000

(Source: *Employment Gazette*, March 1985)

Project

Carry out a survey to discover how the price of an average 'shopping basket' changes over a period of four weeks.

Decide on the contents of your shopping basket. These should be the type of purchases that an average family makes most weeks. It should include some fresh produce as these prices are more likely to change.

Secondly, find the price of each item and calculate the cost of the total 'basket'.

Thirdly, check the prices weekly and make a note of any changes in the cost of individual items and in the total 'basket'.

8.8 Vocabulary

Barter
A system of trade based on the exchange of goods and services.

Base-line
A point of time from which changes will be measured.

Cash
Money in the form of notes and coins which can be used in payment.

Charge card
Similar to a credit card, it can only be used in a particular range of shops.

Cheque
An instruction to a bank to pay some money from a bank account. Usually used to pay for purchases and bills.

Credit
Money in the form of bank lending.

Credit card
A plastic card which can be used to make purchases in a wide variety of shops. All spending is charged to the user's account.

Face value
The value that is shown on a note or coin as the value it has in any exchange.

Insurance premium
The amount that is paid to gain insurance cover against the risks listed in the insurance policy.

CHAPTER 9

POLITICS AND GOVERNMENT

Social groups often need to make decisions. Friends discuss where they will go and what they will do. They are unlikely to take a vote on whether to go to the cinema or to a disco but they will probably do what the majority decide.

When groups are larger, with many members, decisions will be made differently. The members of a youth club will elect a committee which will make decisions on behalf of everyone else. If the members do not like the way the committee run the club they can turn them out and elect others.

When decisions have to be made for whole towns, large companies, or even the nation, it needs far more than an elected committee. Making decisions and carrying them out will become a full-time job for many people. Those who make decisions become very powerful. What they decide can affect the lives of millions of ordinary people.

Politics is about making decisions. It is also about the power of people and groups to make those decisions.

Government decisions affect everyone. The people who make those decisions have tremendous power. Few people ever have total power. In the modern state, power is limited by rights which restrict the use of power. The rights of the individual are recognised in law.

9.1   Governing the country

At one time it was the king or the queen who ruled the country, often helped by the nobles and other powerful individuals. As Parliament gained greater influence the day-to-day work was left to ministers. The most important of these was the Prime, or first, Minister.

The old traditions of the monarchy still continue. It is the Queen who opens Parliament at the start of each session. Ministers are still known as 'Ministers of the Crown'. Every law passed by Parliament still needs the 'Royal Assent'. Parliament still includes a House of Lords, many of whose members are the descendants of the nobles who once advised the monarch.

In reality, however, the powers of the monarch today are not great. Power has passed to Parliament and its elected members who make up the House of Commons. The House of Lords has also changed. As well as the hereditary peers, who inherited their power, there are life peers who are appointed for their own lifetimes. They cannot pass their titles to their descendants.

Government

Most modern systems of government can be divided into three parts. These are known as the legislature, executive and judiciary.

In Britain, Parliament is the *legislature*. Its jobs is to legislate, or pass laws. It decides on the policies which will have to be followed in the day-to-day running of the country. This is carried out by the *executive* which includes the government and the civil service. The Prime Minister leads the government. Although appointed by the monarch, the Prime Minister is usually leader of the political party which has a majority of MPs in the House of Commons.

The civil service

The day-to-day work of the executive is carried out by the civil service, which is divided into a number of departments or ministries. The Treasury is in charge of the nation's finances. The Foreign Office looks after relationships with other countries. The Home Office is concerned with the police and with other 'home' affairs. There are also departments to look after health and social security, trade and industry, education and science, transport, and the other areas of government.

Figure 9.1

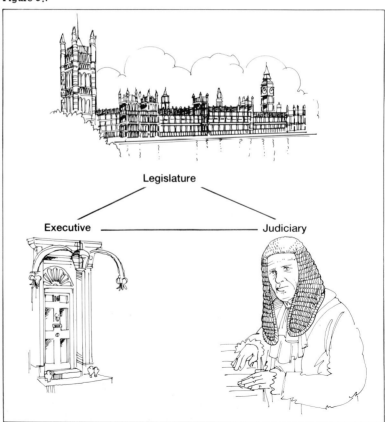

The Cabinet

In charge of each government department there is a minister or, with the larger departments, a Secretary of State. The Home Secretary is the minister who is responsible for the Home Office while the Foreign Secretary is in charge of the Foreign Office. Ministers are chosen by the Prime Minister from the government's supporters in Parliament. The Prime Minister and the other leading ministers make up the Cabinet which meets regularly at 10 Downing Street, the Prime Minister's official residence. The Prime Minister chairs Cabinet meetings. It is in the Cabinet that the government's policies are decided.

Although they are often described as 'Ministers of the Crown', members of the government are responsible not to the monarch but to Parliament. In this way the power of the government is kept under control. Ministers cannot do just what they want. They must answer to Parliament and to those who elected them. For each government department, Parliament has 'select committees' of MPs who keep a watch on the government's activities.

The government must also obey the law. Any citizen, who believes that a minister has acted beyond the powers granted by Parliament, can take the minister to court and eventually to those judges who are members of the House of Lords. These make up the *judiciary*.

Questions

1. What part does the monarch play in the government of the country?
2. What does the title 'Prime Minister' mean?
3. Why is there a civil service?
4. Who makes up the Cabinet?
5. What can the ordinary citizen do if he or she believes that the government has broken the law?
6. In England the rights of the individual were first written down in a document called Magna Carta. Today rights are contained in many different laws. How would you finish the following sentence?
   'Everyone has the right to ...'

The 1978 Labour government in the Cabinet Room at 10 Downing Street.

9.2   American government

America is governed very differently from Britain. Although America is one nation it is made up of 50 separate states. Each state has its own laws, its own system of government and is able to raise its own taxes. The United States of America is a federation of states with its federal government in the city of Washington.

The Constitution

The way America is governed is laid down in the Constitution of the United States of America. This document was written by the Founding Fathers over 200 years ago. There have been a number of Amendments to the Constitution since then. The Constitution not only lays down how the country will be governed but it also protects the rights of the individual.

The Constitution of the United States of America was signed by the Founding Fathers in 1787.

The President

The convention chooses a Democratic candidate to run for President.

Instead of a monarchy, with a king or queen as Head of State, and a Parliament, with a Prime Minister, the writers of the American Constitution decided to have a President.

The President of the United States is the nation's chief executive and is elected every four years. No one may be elected President more than twice so the longest a President can serve is eight years. The President is also Commander-in-Chief of the armed forces.

The election of the President starts more than a year before the new President is due to take office, when the first candidates announce their intention of standing for election. To have any chance of being elected a candidate needs to gain the nomination of one of the two main political parties: the Republicans or the Democrats. In many states the supporters of each party vote to decide which candidates they will support at the national conventions. These elections are known as 'The Primaries' and take place in the two months before the national conventions.

To an outsider the convention seems more like a circus than a political event. There are bands and streamers, bright banners and lots of noise. Leading politicians and show business personalities make speeches while the candidates try to collect the votes of as many delegates as possible. By the end of the convention the party will have decided on its candidate for President and the 'running mate' who will stand for Vice-President.

The election takes place in November. As well as voting for the President each elector is likely to be asked to vote for state governors, senators, mayors, and even the local chief of police.

In practice the voters do not vote for the President. Instead they elect people from their State to serve on an electoral college. It is the electoral college which elects the President.

Congress

Congress is made up of two Houses whose members are elected from each of the states. Members of the House of Representatives are elected for two years whereas members of the Senate serve for six years. The Senate is smaller but far more powerful. Together the two Houses make up the legislative with the power to make laws.

Congress also keeps a check on the activities of the President, many of whose decisions must have Congress' approval.

The Supreme Court

The Supreme Court of nine judges is the guardian of the Constitution. It is the judiciary, and is there to make sure that no one acts against the rules laid down in the Constitution. Although the judges in the Supreme Court are appointed by the President, they cannot be removed. They are appointed for life and are independent of the other sections of the government.

Figure 9·2

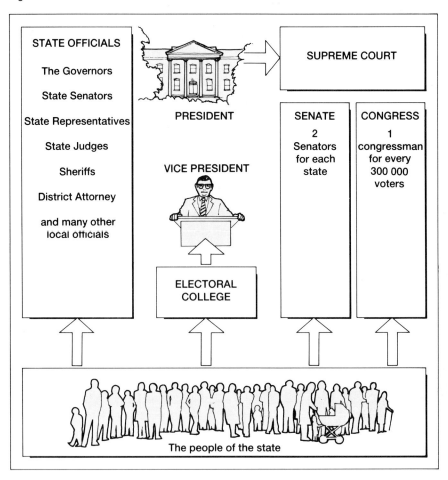

STATE OFFICIALS

The Governors

State Senators

State Representatives

State Judges

Sheriffs

District Attorney

and many other
local officials

PRESIDENT

VICE PRESIDENT

ELECTORAL
COLLEGE

SUPREME COURT

SENATE
2
Senators
for each
state

CONGRESS
1
congressman
for every
300 000
voters

The people of the state

Questions
1. In what ways is the position of President different from that of the British Prime Minister?
2. How are the candidates chosen for election as President of the United States?
3. Who actually elects the President?
4. What are the two Houses of Congress? In what ways are they different?
5. The American system is made up of a number of 'checks and balances'. Which groups keep a check on the actions of the President?

9.3 Elections

Elections take place in many ways. School teams elect their captains, clubs elect their committees, trade unions elect their officers and company shareholders elect the directors. Voting in elections may be organised in various ways. In Britain a 'first-past-the-post' system is used. The person who gets the most votes gets elected even if more people voted for other candidates. In other countries in Europe, voting is by *proportional representation*. Each party's proportion of the total votes decides how many seats the party will receive.

Although most attention is given to general elections when people stand for election to Parliament, this is only one of a number of occasions when people go to the polls.

Many people who would not think of standing for MP can put themselves forward as candidates in local elections. They stand for parish councils, county councils, district and borough councils. There are also elections for the European Parliament.

Sometimes an election has to be held when an MP or local councillor dies or retires. These *by-elections* can often be very important. They provide an opportunity for a government to test its popularity with the voters without having to go to a full general election.

During an election schools and other public buildings are used as polling stations.

General election

Parliament must be re-elected every five years. The Prime Minister may call an election before the five years are up. If the government is defeated on a 'vote of confidence' in the House of Commons a general election must be held.

Anyone who is over 21 and can find 20 people to sign the nomination forms can stand for Parliament. Each candidate must pay a deposit. This is meant to prevent people who are not serious candidates from standing in the election.

To stand a real chance of being elected as a councillor or as an MP you would probably need to be adopted as the candidate of one of the main political parties. Fighting an election can be an expensive business. The party provides a way of raising the money. The local party also helps to do the work that is involved in an election. There may be a full-time election agent who organises everything, party workers who go around knocking on doors, stuffing leaflets in envelopes, putting-up posters and arranging meetings.

Each party has a manifesto which tells the voters what the party will do if it wins the election. This enables the voters to compare the different parties before making up their minds.

On election day the polling stations open early in the morning. Each registered elector votes by marking the ballot paper. This is done in secret and the marked ballot is placed in a sealed box.

Party workers will try to get as many people to the polls as possible. When the polls close and the vote has been taken everyone waits for the result. The candidate who gets the largest number of votes wins and is declared Member of Parliament for the constituency.

In a general election the same events take place all over the country as results are declared. Counting the votes may go on right through the night and people watching at home on the television will see the results for each party gradually mount up. In 1987 there were 650 MPs to be elected. The party which wins more than half of the total seats has the majority in Parliament and forms the government.

In some elections no single party wins enough seats to get a majority. When this happens the leaders of the largest parties must try to get support from some of the smaller parties so that they can form a government. When this happens there is said to be 'a hung Parliament'.

Discussion

Using Figure 9.4, decide whether the following statements are true or false. What evidence do you base your decision on?

Figure 9.3

	True	False	Evidence
1. To be elected as a government a political party must have a majority of the votes in the election			
2. The Conservative Party is the only party since 1974 that has received more than half of the votes cast in a general election			
3. The Liberal/SDP Alliance may have won 25% of the votes but they won less than 4% of the seats in Parliament			
4. Since 1974 the smaller parties have not only increased their share of the votes but have also won more seats			
5. A political party could see its share of the votes fall but still win more seats in the House of Commons			

Figure 9·4 General elections: voting and seats by main parties 1964–1983

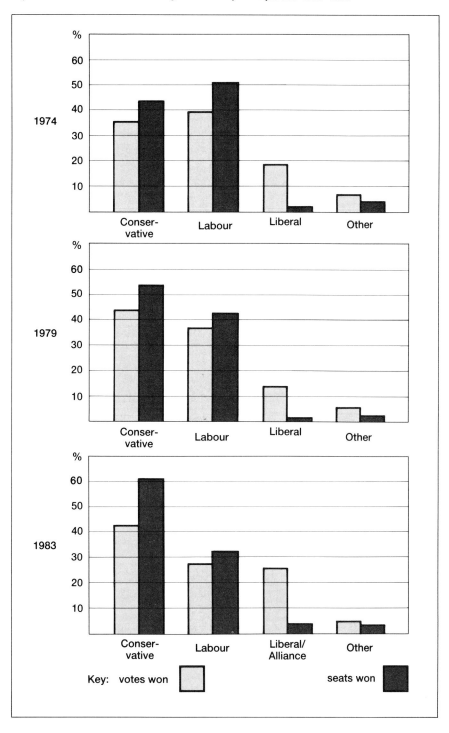

9.4   Voting

In an election most people know how they will vote long before the election is called. How someone votes is linked to their attitudes on many other issues. It is affected by their job, by their social class and the groups to which they belong. Regular support for a political party is known as *partisanship*.

At one time it was thought that you could tell how someone would vote simply from their social class. People thought that all of the working classes voted for the Labour Party and the middle classes voted Conservative. It is not difficult to see why this could never have been true. If all manual workers and their families always voted Labour then the Labour Party would never lose an election. It clearly does not work that way. Many manual workers vote Conservative just as many middle class voters vote Labour.

Another problem arises when we realise that since the middle of the 1970s voters have had other parties to choose from and have frequently voted for 'third parties'. These do not seem to have the same links to social class that Labour and Conservative once had.

The idea of partisanship based on social class will not fit the facts. The old class-based pattern of voting has changed and new patterns have developed. People are more likely to vote on the issues in an election, choosing the party which they think will do the best job or will give them the best deal. They are more likely to be influenced by the views expressed at work or in the local community.

All of these changes mean that it is now more difficult to predict how people will vote.

Opinion polls and voting trends

As well as changes in voting patterns, which may take place over many years, there are also changes which take place from month to month. These changes make up the *voting trend*. Most people make up their minds on politics and keep to it. They don't change their views very often. There are some people who do change their ideas and some, such as new voters, who have not yet had to decide how to vote. Those who switch their votes from one party to another are known as '*floating voters*'.

Discovering how people intend to vote is the job of the opinion polls. These 'political surveys' are being carried out all of the time. A typical poll will ask as many as a thousand voters questions like 'Who do you think would make the best Prime Minister?' and 'If there were an election tomorrow who would you vote for?' These polls give an indication of the voting trend. They measure the popularity of political parties and their leaders.

Figure 9.5

Poll keeps Tories in first place

THE Conservative Party's comfortable lead in the opinion polls is confirmed yet again by a survey published today.

The Gallup poll in The Daily Telegraph gives Mrs Thatcher an 11.5 per cent head start with 40.5 per cent of public support - half a point short of the figure the Prime Minister is reported to want established before calling a General Election.

The Labour Party has once again been placed third, one point behind the Alliance's 29 per cent.

June is now hot favourite to be General Election month, says Bookmakers William Hill. It has shortened its price from 6-4 to Evens, with the Tories 1-5 to win.

June Fever, page 6

(Source: *London Daily News*, 16 April 1987)

Alliance pushing hard to move into second place

Polls give flying start to Thatcher

GUARDIAN MARPLAN INDEX

(Source: The *Guardian*, 14 May 1987)

Polls can have bad effects. They can influence the way the election turns out. If one party is predicted to be heading for an easy win its supporters might become apathetic and not bother to vote. The other parties, however, might work even harder and try to capture those extra votes needed. In some countries polls are not allowed in the weeks leading up to an election.

Project

Opinion polls cover issues as well as personalities. Local polls are often used to discover people's views on such issues as local health services, the buses, re-development plans, leisure provision or shopping facilities.

Choose an important local issue and conduct an opinion poll to discover what people's views are. If your poll is to be of any use it must be carefully planned, taking care to test out the questions in a 'pilot survey'. You will need to devise a way to get an accurate sample and your interviewers will need some training. Your conclusions should be written up in a report, presenting the evidence and giving your conclusions.

9.5   Members of Parliament

Most MPs sit on the backbenches. The 'frontbenches' of the House of
Commons are where the Prime Minister, the Cabinet and the leaders
of the opposition party sit. An MP who belongs to one of the smaller
parties will sit at the end of the chamber on the 'crossbenches'.

An MP is elected to represent the people of a *constituency*. When
matters which are likely to effect the constituency are being discussed,
MPs are expected to put the views of the people they represent. As
well as representing the constituency as a whole, MPs deal with the
problems of individual constituents, writing letters to ministers,
contacting government departments and arranging any help that is
needed.

Only part of MP's time is taken up with constituency business. Many MPs have their own interests and will spend some of their time working on those. One MP may be concerned with the welfare of children, or the disabled. Another may be an expert on defence or trade with south-east Asia. It is quite usual for MPs to be employed by organisations to represent their concerns in Parliament. Business concerns and trade unions often sponsor MPs to act on their behalf. When this happens the MP concerned must declare it so that everyone knows that they have an interest.

Figure 9·6 The diary of an MP

Sunday	Monday	Tuesday	Wednesday	Thursday	Friday	Saturday
2-00 Attend weekend conference of local party	9.30 Answer letters from constituents	9-45 Worked on speech on unemployment	10-30 Meeting with experts on unemployment	9-30 Worked on correspondence	9-00 Tour of new factory sites in constituency	10-00 Surgery for constituents
	10-30 Meeting with local party agent	11-00 Meeting at Department of Employment	12-00 Lunch with chairman of constituency party	12-00 Spoke at meeting on unemployment	11-30 Spoke to sixth form conference	2-00 Opened Red Cross bazaar
	12-00 Lunch with Chamber of Commerce	2-30 House of Commons for question time	2-30 Standing committee on Protection of Animals Bill	2-30 House of Commons for question time	1-00 Lunch with head teachers of local schools	
	2-00 Train to London, finish off letters	4-00 Meeting with local trade union delegation	6-00 House of Commons for votes on Industry Bill	5-30 Caught train to constituency	3-00 Meeting at civic centre with the mayor and councillors	
	5-00 House of Commons for debate on Police Bill	7-00 House of Commons for debate on Industry Bill	8-00 Meeting of backbench MPs	8-30 Public meeting in constituency	7-30 Local party meeting	
	8-15 Dinner with visitors from constituency	10-00 Voted and went home	10-35 Final votes on Industry Bill	11-00 Back home went to bed		
	10-45 Vote in House		12-30 Back to flat, bed!			
	11-50 Back to London flat, to bed					

Being a Member of Parliament also means that you are involved in the work of Parliament. There will be debates to attend. Ministers will need to be asked questions in 'question time'. Most MPs are also members of a party and will vote with the party in debates and on important bills. Some of the MPs in each party have the job of making sure that all of the MPs in the party vote correctly. They are known as the 'whips'. On very important issues there will be a 'three-line whip' which means that every MP must vote with the party.

Not all of the work of Parliament takes place in 'the Chamber', as the House of Commons is sometimes called. There are committees to attend. *Standing committees* deal with new laws while *select committees* keep a check on important areas of government business.

An important part of the work of Parliament involves making laws.

Most new laws begin as a *bill* which is presented to the House of Commons. When Parliament debates a bill it is called a *reading*. The first reading of a bill is a fairly formal affair. The title of the bill is read out and there is not much debate. The second reading is a more lengthy affair which can go on over a number of days. Once the main outline has been agreed the bill goes to a standing committee for the committee stage. The exact details of new law are worked out and amendments are made. Finally, it returns to the House of Commons for a third reading when the amendments are either accepted or rejected. The bill is now ready to 'go upstairs' to the House of Lords.

The same process is repeated in the Lords, though any changes that the Lords make to a bill must be agreed by a vote in the House of Commons. Finally when the bill has been through all of the stages it is sent to the Queen for 'the Royal Assent'. At this point it becomes an Act of Parliament.

Although it often appears to be the government that runs the country it is Parliament which has the final say. No government can function without the support of Parliament. Ministers and civil servants must therefore answer to Parliament for their actions.

Questions
1. Which MPs would sit:
   a on the government frontbench?
   b on the crossbenches?
   c on the backbenches?
2. Why do the parties have 'whips'?
3. Parliament has two types of committee. What are they for?
4. What does the MPs diary tell you about:
   a the MP's special interests?
   b committees attended?
   c time spent in London and time spent in the constituency?

9.6   Making decisions about the economy

In any economy decisions have to be made about what to produce and how to produce it. In some countries the government makes the decisions centrally. Where decisions are made in this way we would say that the country has a planned economy. Russia, China and other communist societies have *planned economies*.

In other countries these decisions are left to industry. Decisions are made on the basis of what people want. This system is known as a *market economy*. Demand influences what is produced and the prices that people will pay. Instead of being owned by the state, firms are owned by private individuals. This is sometimes known as a system of *private enterprise*.

Britain has both of these systems. There are firms which are owned privately and others which are owned by the state. The state allows the market to determine prices for most goods but may also fix prices for certain basic items such as milk and bread. The government provides grants and subsidies to encourage firms to move to areas of high unemployment. There are also laws which protect the health and safety of workers and which give workers their basic rights.

The British economy is, therefore, a *mixed economy* with both private enterprise and some central control and state involvement.

The Budget

As well as decisions about the way industry will operate, the government has to make decisions about what needs to be done and where the money will come from. These decisions centre on the Budget.

The Chancellor of the Exchequer, on his way to present his Budget to the House of Commons, holds up the 'Budget Box' used by every Chancellor since Gladstone's Budget of 1860.

On Budget Day the Chancellor of the Exchequer presents to Parliament the government's plans for the British economy. Most of the people listening to the Budget news on radio or television will want to know how the proposals will affect them individually. How much tax will they have to pay? How much will be added to the price of a gallon of petrol or a pint of beer?

Taxation

Everyone pays taxes in some form or another. Wage-earners pay taxes on what they earn. Shoppers pay taxes on what they buy. Companies pay taxes on their profits. People who smoke and drink pay duty on cigarettes, beer and wine.

Some of these are direct taxes which the government collects directly from the people who pay them. Income tax is collected through a system

Figure 9·8 The 1986 Budget

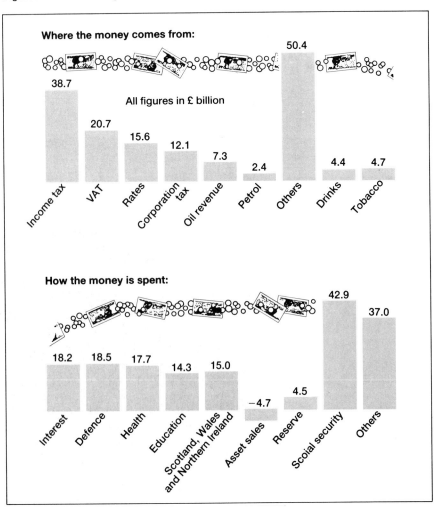

Where the money comes from:

All figures in £ billion

Income tax	VAT	Rates	Corporation tax	Oil revenue	Petrol	Others	Drinks	Tobacco
38.7	20.7	15.6	12.1	7.3	2.4	50.4	4.4	4.7

How the money is spent:

Interest	Defence	Health	Education	Scotland, Wales and Northern Ireland	Asset sales	Reserve	Scoial security	Others
18.2	18.5	17.7	14.3	15.0	−4.7	4.5	42.9	37.0

known as PAYE, or Pay As You Earn. It is collected even before the wage-earner receives his or her pay-packet. Other taxes are indirect. The government collects these from manufacturers or retailers who then pass the costs on to the customer. Value Added Tax (VAT) is an indirect tax which is charged on many goods and services. Excise duty is a tax which is charged on petrol, alcohol and tobacco.

Taxes not only provide the government with money. They are also linked to the government's social and economic policies. Cigarettes, for example, are very heavily taxed. Heart and lung diseases, directly caused by smoking, cost the country millions of pounds each year. The tax on tobacco not only earns money for the government, it also makes smoking expensive and discourages people from smoking.

The Chancellor could, if he wished, place a tax on almost anything. In the past taxes have been levied on salt, windows or, with the poll tax, even people. In reality, methods of taxation must be chosen very carefully. A good tax should be easy to understand, simple to collect, difficult for people to avoid paying and fair. When the Chancellor places a tax on goods it is important there are no alternative products which might be purchased instead.

Discussion: planning the Budget

Managing the economy can be difficult. Changes in one part of the national economy will have effects on other parts. If consumers have to pay more taxes they will have less to spend on goods and will demand higher wages. If people spend their savings on imported goods there will be less demand for home-produced goods and less to invest in new factories.

Imagine that you are a government committee considering proposals for the coming budget. What would be the effect of carrying out each of the following proposals?

1. Increase income tax by 5p in the £ to pay for a programme of new hospitals and motorway building.
2. Use the Bank of England to push up interest rates to encourage people to put more of their money into savings.
3. Increase government borrowing to raise money for schools, new leisure centres and the arts.
4. Make a large cut in income tax and increase the level of all state benefits.

9.7 The Legislation Game

To play the Legislation Game you need dice and some counters. You begin in the Members' lobby where you wait to hear the result of the ballot . . .

Figure 9·7 The legislation game

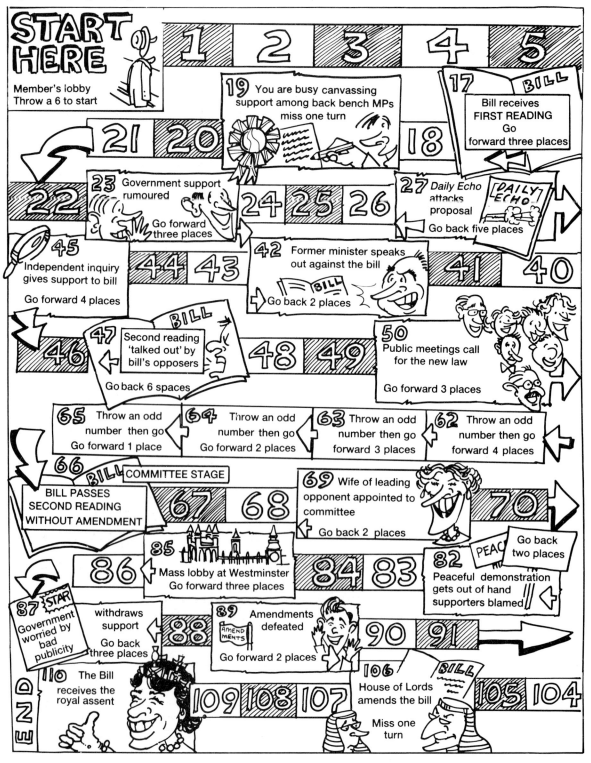

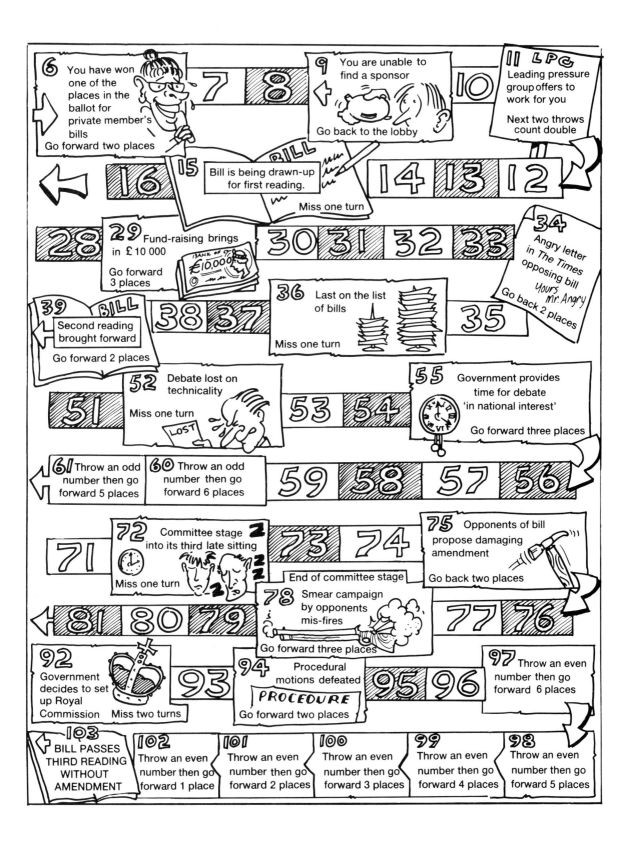

9.8　Local councils

In every part of Britain there are councils which provide services for the local area.

In the larger cities these are borough or district councils and they provide most of the local services. The remaining services are provided by various boards and agencies which cover the whole city or region.

Over the rest of the country there are a number of *tiers*, or levels, of local government. The job of providing local services is shared between the different tiers. The 'top tier' authority is the County. In Scotland they are known as Regions and in Northern Ireland they come under Education and Library Boards. There are 39 County Councils in England and Wales, 10 Regions in Scotland and 5 Boards in Northern Ireland. These Counties, Regions and Boards can then be divided into over 350 districts. In many places there are also parish, town or community councils. There are over 11 000 of these.

Each local authority has a council made up of local people who have been elected for a period of four years. In the larger authorities, being a councillor is almost a full-time job but the majority of councillors carry out their duties in their spare time.

Ad hoc authorities

Not all of the services are provided by elected local authorities. Some services can only be provided over a very large area. These are provided by *ad hoc* bodies set up to provide a particular service. Hospitals, for example, are provided by seventeen Regional Health Authorities.

Figure 9.9 Structure of local councils

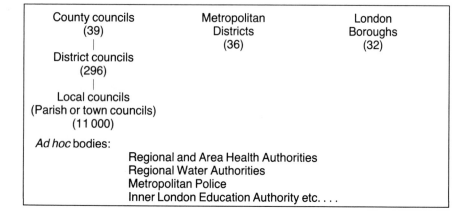

Figure 9·10 Where the money comes from (sources of income
for a typical county council)

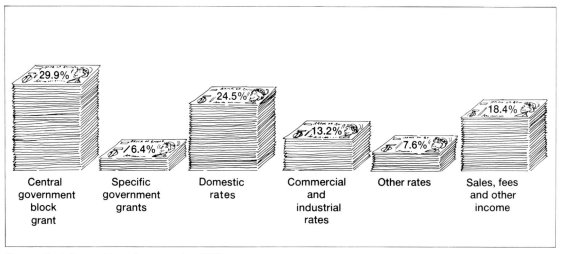

(Source: Kent County Council rates notice, 1986)

Figure 9·11 Local government services

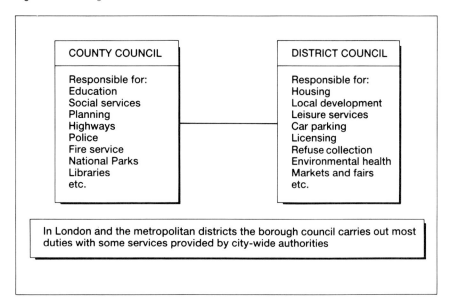

The local council is responsible for a number of important services.
It may run schools and colleges, provide council houses, build and
maintain the roads, collect household refuse and run the fire brigade.
Many of the council's duties are required by law.

A typical local council is made up of a number of departments. Within
each of these departments there are local government officers who carry
out the day-to-day work of the council. These officers are similar to civil
servants but they work for local government.

Each department is responsible to a committee of the council. These committees are made up of a number of elected councillors.

The work of the council is paid for from a tax on all local property (this is called a *rate*), and by a grant from the government. Councils also charge for some of their services.

Table 9.1   County rates

Income	£million	Expenditure	£million
Government grants	258.00	Education	344.70
Domestic rates	140.20	Police	64.50
Commercial rates	50.50	Social services	62.40
Industrial rates	26.70	Highways	70.70
Other rates	41.40	Fire	16.70
Sales, fees etc.	105.30	Libraries	9.10
		Planning	2.70
		Waste disposal	4.80
		Magistrates courts	4.20
		Other services	21.40
		Contingency fund	20.90
Total	622.10		622.10

Questions
1. What is the main source of the council's income?
2. How much money comes from the ordinary domestic ratepayers in the county?
3. What percentage of the rates is paid by commerce and industry?
4. Which of the council services takes up most of the money?
5. A very cold winter could cause more damage to the roads than would have been expected. The county's highways budget could easily be used up. Where would they get the extra money to mend the roads without cutting back other services?

9.9   Making yourself heard

One way of looking at politics is to think of it as a number of inputs and outputs. The outputs are the decisions made by the government and by local councils. Before those decisions can be made the politicians and civil servants have to take account of the inputs.

Inputs come from many sources. There is information from the government's own departments on how well the country is running, where there are problems and what needs to be done. There is also information from other groups in the country who tell the government what it ought to be doing. Some of this comes through the political parties and some through pressure groups. The newspapers and television are another important source of information.

Figure 9·12 Input and outputs

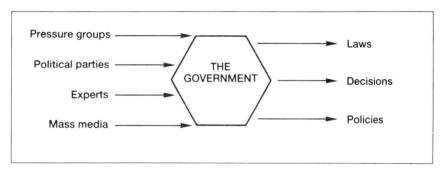

Political parties

Each party is like a giant pyramid. At the top are the party leaders. They are usually elected. The base of the pyramid is made up of many thousands of ordinary party members. Some of these are members in

Figure 9·13 The party pyramid

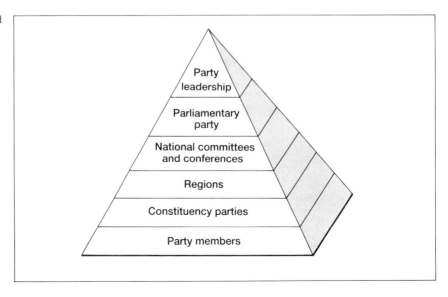

name only. They pay their subscriptions and do their bit to help in elections but are not involved in other party activities. Other members are more active. They attend branch meetings. They may be local officers of the party, perhaps standing as local councillors. Some of these *activists* will represent their branch on regional committees and may go as delegates to the regional or national conferences.

The various groups will help to decide on party policies, debating what needs to be done and how the party can best plan for the future. When a party is in government the pyramid of local, regional and national groups will keep ministers in touch with the views of the 'grass roots' members. When a party is in opposition it will help to shape the party's policies for the next election.

Pressure groups

An individual who wants to influence a government decision often has great difficulty in being listened to. When people get together to form a group they can do much more. A group can organise itself to influence government decisions. Such groups are often known as *pressure groups* because they put pressure on those who make decisions. They may also be known as *interest groups* because they represent people with particular interests.

Some groups aim to promote a particular issue. They may want to build new roads or change the law on alcohol. These are *promotional* groups. Other groups seek to protect things. It may be that they want to preserve the countryside or protect the working conditions of long-distance lorry drivers. These are *protectional* groups.

A pressure group may appear quite suddenly to take action on a particular cause. Parents may get together to put pressure on the council to provide a crossing patrol on a busy road. Local residents may try to prevent the building of a new airport, or a motorway. When they have achieved their aims they will disband. Other groups, however, are more permanent. They have developed as organisations with paid employees and regular contact with government. These are sometimes known as *lobbies* because they 'lobby' (or talk to) MPs in the corridors (or lobbies) of the Palace of Westminster.

Womens' groups campaign against proposals to place tighter controls on abortion.

The methods used by a pressure group depend upon the amount of power and influence that a group has. If the group is accepted as representing an important section of society and has strong links with government, its work will be relatively easy. If, on the other hand, the group is kept outside of government it will have to use many more methods to put its point-of-view across. Protests and demonstrations, publicity in newspapers and on television, petitions and campaigns will be needed if it is to influence the government.

CASE STUDY

The road lobby

The 'road lobby' is an example of a powerful and well organised pressure group. It is made up of a number of groups which have an interest in road transport. They have an important influence on the government's approach to transport and road-building.

Although it has had great influence on the government it does not represent all road users. Pedestrians and cyclists are not part of the road lobby. Those who live near to main roads are not part of it either.

The road lobby puts pressure on the government in a number of ways. On some issues, such as the proposal to nationalise road transport, public campaigns are launched in the press and on television. On other issues it may seek to persuade ministers or senior civil servants. This may be linked to lobbying MPs from all political parties. Campaigns may also be organised at the local level through local newspapers. Local councils may be the target for pressure as well as central government.

Figure 9·14 The road lobby

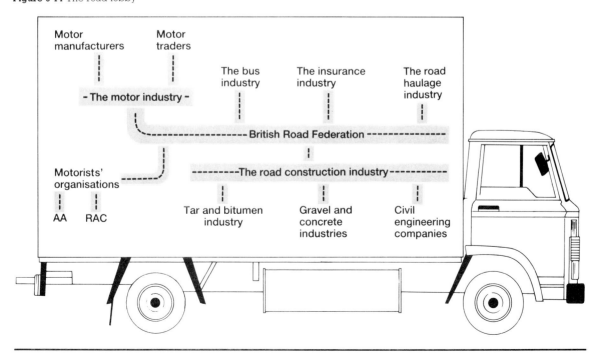

9.10 Vocabulary

By-election	An election which is called following the death or resignation of the elected MP or local councillor.
Constituency	A district which elects an MP.
Direct tax	A tax which is paid directly by the tax-payer.
Indirect tax	A tax which is passed on to the tax-payer in the prices that they pay for goods and services.
Interest group	A group or organisation which represents a particular set of interests.
Manifesto	The document published by a political party before an election which lists the party's aims.
Monarchy	Rule by an hereditary ruler, such as a king or queen.
Poll	An election or a survey of public opinion.
Pressure group	Another name for an interest group.
Proportional representation	An electoral system in which the result is decided in 'proportion' to the votes cast for each party.
Ward	An area of a local district or county which elects a number of councillors. A part of a constituency.

CHAPTER 10

CRIME AND DEVIANCE

You are watching two people playing a game. Scattered around the board on black and white squares are a number of strangely shaped objects. The players take turns to move these objects from place to place on the board. Sometimes they remove them completely.

As you watch you realise that different shapes are moved in different ways. Some are moved slowly, a little at a time. Others make long moves right across the table. There are objects that move diagonally and some that move along the lines of the squares.

What you have been watching is a game of chess and as you watch it you begin to understand the rules of the game.

Social life is not very different from such a game. People behave in ways which can usually be expected. We recognise patterns in their behaviour. How you behave often depends on who you are and where you are. At a football match everyone will clap and shout, singing chants to urge their team on. You would not normally behave like that in church!

Most of our actions are, in some way, affected by rules. Some of these are formal rules, written down as laws and by-laws. Many of them are just accepted as part of everyday life. We may not even think of them as rules. When we say that someone is 'polite', or has 'good manners' we are saying that he or she knows how to behave according to a certain set of rules. These rules are sometimes known as *etiquette*.

The game of chess has its own set of formal rules. Without them a game of chess could never begin. You cannot change the rules of chess whenever you feel like it or make up your own rules and still expect it to be chess. In the same way there are formal rules which control what people can do in everyday life. The most important of these are laws passed by the state.

Everyday life is not the same as a game of chess. The rules do change. There are different expectations in different situations. People do behave in different ways without life coming to a stop. Yet there is also order in life. Things are not totally unpredictable.

The way this social order comes into being is of interest to social scientists.

10.1   Social rules

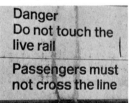

Our everyday lives follow a pattern. If they didn't we would find it difficult to know what to do. We know what to expect and come to recognise the behaviour that fits any situation. This is part of the process of *socialisation*. When we find ourselves in new situations we have to learn new ways to behave. This happens when you go to a new school or start a job.

Social rules are often informal. People accept them without the need for them to be written down as laws. Customs, conventions and fashion are informal rules. Sociologists refer to these as *social norms, mores* or *folkways*.

There is no punishment for breaking or for ignoring these informal rules. You will not be thrown into prison for using the wrong titles when speaking to a bishop or for not wearing fashionable clothes. You may be regarded by others as *deviant* or as anti-social.

Informal social rules and codes of behaviour are enforced by social pressure. These can be an important influence on how you behave. What other people might think or say can be an important form of social control. Social pressure is a very powerful way of enforcing informal rules and of making people conform.

When people come together into organised groups formal rules become more important. Games have written rules. Clubs and societies have their rule books. These rules only affect those who play the game or belong to the club. In any organised activity there will be formal and informal rules.

Crime and deviance

There are some rules that effect everyone. These are rules laid down by the state as *laws*. The state makes the laws and uses the police and courts to enforce them.

If you go against the informal social rules of custom or fashion you may be viewed as non-conformist or as deviant. Breaking the state's rules means committing a *crime*. Crime is behaviour which breaks the law. Crime is also often seen as deviant. You can be deviant without becoming a criminal. Most people would agree that going to school every day dressed as a gorilla is deviant. It is not a crime. It could only become a crime if the state passed a law forbidding it. It may, of course, be against the school rules!

Whether an activity is seen as normal or as deviant does not depend on anyone passing a law. It depends on how groups and individuals view the activity. Often behaviour which is deviant for one group of people is quite acceptable for others. Deviance can be said to be relative because it depends on the situation and the groups concerned.

The queue

If you wanted a ticket for the Australian Rules World Series football matches in Melbourne in 1967 you would have had to queue. Some people started queuing six days before the ticket offices opened. The queue developed its own set of rules and customs.

All queues are based on the principle of 'first come, first served'. People at the back of the queue have less chance of getting a ticket than those at the front. This is one of the unwritten rules of the queue which everyone understands.

In the Melbourne queue you did not have to stand in line for all of the time. Queuers could take 'time out'. A short 'time out' could be taken just by leaving a coat or bag to mark your place in the queue. For a longer period you would need someone else to 'stand' for you. Some groups queued in shifts, taking it in turns to queue for other people.

Queuing is a form of work. It takes time and a great deal of effort. At the end you are rewarded with your tickets. Some people tried to get the rewards without doing the work. These were queue-jumpers. People in the queue regarded queue-jumpers as deviants because they would not conform to the principle of 'first-come, first-served'. They were also anti-social because their behaviour had a harmful effect on others by pushing them back in the queue.

Queuers used a variety of methods to control this kind of anti-social activity. They protected themselves by making barriers out of anything that came to hand. On rare occasions physical force was used and fights broke out when people pushed into the front of the queue. More often the queue-jumper would be the target of social pressure. People behind them would make comments, possibly even calling out. They would try to shame the queue-jumper into leaving.

Any queue is an example of a social activity which can develop its own set of rules and customs.

Questions
1. What were the informal rules of the Melbourne queue?
2. What made them 'informal' instead of 'formal' rules?
3. Who were the rules aimed at?
4. How were the rules enforced?

Discussion

Crime is an action which breaks the law. Deviance is behaviour which is against the normally accepted behaviour of a group.

Which of the following actions would you describe as:

a deviant but not criminal;
b criminal and deviant;
c criminal but not generally thought to be deviant;
d neither criminal nor deviant?

Figure 10.1

	Deviant not criminal	Criminal and deviant	Criminal but not thought deviant	Neither criminal nor deviant
1. Robbing a bank in broad daylight				
2. Riding a bicycle without proper lights				
3. Shoplifting				
4. Watching 'Coronation Street' on the television				
5. Buying cigarettes under the age of 16				
6. Getting married underwater				

10.2   The police

Two hundred years ago law and order was enforced by the local Justices of the Peace, assisted by constables and watchmen. As towns and cities grew at the end of the eighteenth century crime also increased. This was the time of the French Revolution. Many people in Britain feared that the mob might also seize power in London and other large cities. This led to the first police force in London in 1829. Police forces were not set up elsewhere until after 1856. Today there are 52 separate police forces in Britain. The largest is the Metropolitan Police Force with 27 000 police officers and 13 000 full-time civilians.

Each police force is under the control of a Chief Constable. Outside of London the Chief Constable is responsible to the local Police Committee. The Metropolitan Police in London are under the Home Secretary. As well as being the police force for London the Metropolitan Police provides many services for the regional forces from its headquarters at New Scotland Yard.

Figure 10·2 The growth of the police force

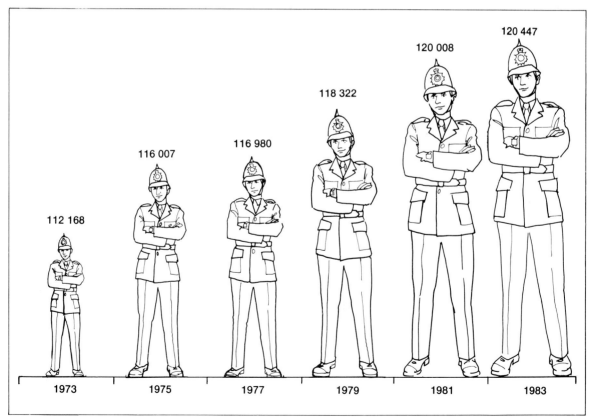

(Source: Annual Abstract 1985, Table 4·2)

The job of the police has changed greatly since 1829. The development of the motor car created the need for traffic control. Modern crime is an international problem often carried-out on a large-scale. New crimes have arisen. The nineteenth-century police were not concerned with crimes like stealing cars or computer-fraud.

Fighting crime

Preventing crime and catching criminals are an important part of police work. It is often easier to prevent a crime than to catch the criminal. Campaigns to encourage people to take more care of their belongings are an important part of crime prevention. The police operate Neighbourhood Watch schemes which encourage people to be on the look-out for anyone acting suspiciously. Local 'home beat' police officers and community police schemes also aim to prevent crime taking place. Crime prevention officers often visit schools to speak to children.

Figure 10·3 Clearing-up crime, England and Wales, 1983

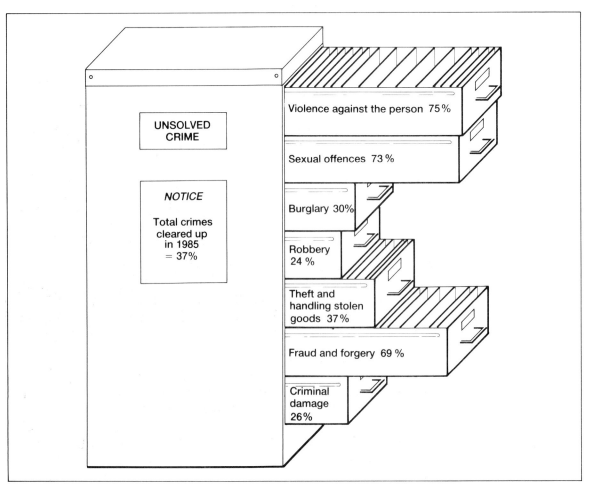

UNSOLVED CRIME

NOTICE

Total crimes cleared up in 1985 = 37%

Violence against the person 75%

Sexual offences 73%

Burglary 30%

Robbery 24%

Theft and handling stolen goods 37%

Fraud and forgery 69%

Criminal damage 26%

(Source: *Social Trends*, 1985)

Catching criminals is the job of the CID, or Criminal Investigation Department. Modern detectives rely on forensic science to help them catch the criminals. Some crimes are easier to solve than others. Fraud has a high clear-up rate because the crime is often only discovered when someone is caught. A large proportion of crimes still remain unsolved.

Keeping the peace

In the days before there were police the army would be used to keep order and to prevent riots.

Today the police will be present at any large gathering whether it is a football match, a big parade or a demonstration. They will be there to keep the peace and to protect property. The Public Order laws give the police the power to control marches and demonstrations.

The use of the police in strikes and demonstrations has caused bitter argument. In order to control crowd violence the police have had to behave more like an army than a police force. They have been described as 'paramilitary'.

A Metropolitan police tactical firearms squad armed with plastic bullets at the Tottenham riots in 1985.

The secret social service

Many people turn to the police when they are in trouble. On an average day the police may be called out to stop a family argument, to quieten a noisy party, to capture escaped animals or to search for a lost child. This is the 'social service' side of police work. In some areas as many as three out of every four calls to the police station are for help in dealing with social problems. Some police officers feel that such things have little to do with 'real police work' and that they take them away from the job of catching criminals.

Traffic and other duties

In some countries the control of motor vehicles and road traffic is separate from the work of police. In Britain there are traffic wardens but they come under the local police force. The work of the traffic police may include escorting lorries with wide loads, helping the injured in motorway accidents and taking over at road junctions when the traffic lights go wrong.

As well as these jobs the police may also license taxi-cabs, keep a check on foreigners living in Britain, guard foreign embassies and supervise polling stations on election days.

Discussion

There are many different sides to the work of the police. Which aspects of police work are shown by the following activities?

Figure 10.4

	Fighting crime	Keeping the peace	Secret social service	Traffic and the motor car
Tracing missing persons				
Controlling football crowds				
Investigating a bank robbery				
Policing a demonstration				
Testing motorists with the breathalyser				
Catching drugs pushers				
Dealing with family arguments				
Preventing road accidents				

10.3   Police work

Life inside an ordinary local police station is very different from the picture shown in television dramas. There is very little of the frantic excitement as criminals are brought in and police officers rush out to answer emergencies. The main activity inside a police station often seems to be filling in forms. Policemen and women spend many hours each day at paperwork. There are books to record who is on duty, to keep a log of each day's events, to note who is in the cells and who has been charged.

Figure 10·5 What do the police do all day? (all figures are percentages)

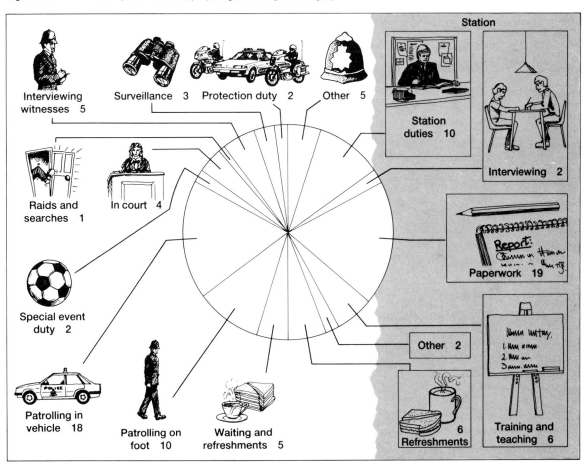

(Source: *Police and People in London*, vol III)

The police station

Each police force is divided into divisions. In a division there are a number of police stations. One of these, usually bigger and better equipped, will be the divisional station. A country district may have the police station attached to the local constable's house. The police station is the police officers 'base camp' where each day's work begins and ends.

Every twenty-four hours is divided into three shifts or 'reliefs'. In charge of each relief there is a duty officer who has the rank of inspector. One sergeant in each station will be responsible for the front office and for charging anyone who has been arrested. Another sergeant will supervise the cells and the prisoners.

The routine work is carried out by the constables. There may be 30 or 40 constables on each relief. In practice very few of these are likely to be available at any one time. Some will be at court while others will be away on leave. Demonstrations or crowd control will take away some more. An average relief may contain less than 20 constables to work in the station and patrol the beats.

Each shift begins with a parade when the various tasks are sorted out. Those inside the police station are dealt with first. Constables from the relief will be allocated to the communications office and to assist the station officer at the front desk. Then officers will be assigned to the cars and to foot patrols. Out of the 20 constables who make up a relief as many as ten could be working inside one of the police stations, four in cars and only six left to walk the beat.

There will also be a number of *home beat officers* who work within a local area. The home beat constable's job is to get to know people in the community and to be recognised as the 'local bobby'. This type of 'community policing' gets the police out of their cars and back on the beat. The home beat officer will visit schools and youth clubs, talking to local people and getting to know the problems in the area.

Community policing schemes bring the police into close contact with the people of the district.

Figure 10·6 Police ranks and badges

Commander

Chief superintendent

Superintendent

Chief inspector

Inspector

Sergeant

Constable

Communications

The communications office is the information centre of the police station. As well as telephones for calls from the general public it contains the radio link to the cars and foot patrols. There are also computer terminals which link the station with the county police headquarters and with the Police National Computer.

In the larger divisional police stations an experienced police officer will have the job of *collator*. This involves checking through each day's charge sheets and reports from constables and home beat officers to find useful information on known criminals. The collator will look for patterns in the crimes that have been reported, possible trouble spots and anything that might be of help either to the relief constables or to the CID.

On an average day there will be far more calls than the police could possibly deal with. The police officers on duty will have to make decisions about the importance and urgency of the different calls and then decide what action to take. If every incident was dealt with the police would not be able to cope.

Specialist police

In many parts of the country the local police can get help in an emergency from specialist police groups. These could include dog-handlers or police frogmen to help on a search as well as armed police or riot squads.

The Criminal Investigation Department, or CID, is responsible for investigating crime. CID officers may be involved in the hunt for a murderer or in the investigation of fraud. Within the CID there are special groups to investigate serious crimes, terrorism and illegal drugs.

Discussion

The duty sergeant in the police station has received the following calls. What order of importance would you put them in? What action should be taken?

a An elderly lady has reported seeing someone climbing over a fence at the rear of her neighbour's house.

b A man has telephoned to say that a kitten is stuck on a branch of a tree and cannot get down.

c Two boys have come into the station to report the theft of a bicycle.

d A woman has reported hearing screams coming from a nearby house.

e A car has crashed into a lamp-post near the High Street. No one is hurt.

f A number of people have telephoned to say that the burglar alarm is ringing at a warehouse on the industrial estate.

g Someone has broken into an empty house and the neighbours think it may be squatters.

h A shopkeeper has been attacked and the till robbed.

10.4   Measuring crime

Can we believe what we read in the newspapers? How do we know
that crime is increasing? Where do we get evidence about the amount
of crime that is taking place?

Most people are unlikely to have personal experience of crime. An
average household can expect to be burgled once every forty years
or have a car stolen once every sixty years. Our knowledge of crime
comes largely from what we read in the newspaper or see on television.

Criminal statistics are based on information from the police and from
the courts. The police keep a record of crimes that have been reported
while the courts know the number of people convicted and sentenced.
Neither of these sources of evidence tell us about the number of crimes
that are actually committed.

Lord Chief Justice warns of huge crime wave

The lawless Eighties...

STANDARDS LOWERED 'AT EVERY STAGE AND AT EVERY LEVEL'

One major offence every ten seconds

Serious crime hits new peak

The 'dark figure'

Many more crimes take place than are reported to the police. A number
of those that are reported may not be recorded. There will always be
a 'dark figure' of unreported crime. The social scientist's problem is to
know how large that 'dark figure' is.

People fail to report crimes for many reasons. They may think that
the crime is too trivial or that there is no point in reporting it because
nothing will be done. Often the person who commits a crime is known

to the victim who may be reluctant to report it. The victim may not want to get a friend in trouble or may fear what else might happen if the police are informed.

Reporting a crime may also depend on who the victim is. Not all of the victims of crime are individuals. Some may be organisations. Stealing from an employer, shoplifting, or not paying your fare on the buses are crimes against organisations. Some crimes do not have victims and there is no one to report that a crime has taken place. Drug abuse, for example, only affects the drug user. There is often no one else involved and therefore no one to report the crime. Finally, some crimes may not be detected. If they are not detected then they will not be reported.

Moral panic

The number of crimes reported to the police and put on record depends on what the public and the police think is important. Newspapers and television can make people more aware of certain crimes. Particular crimes can become 'news'. People will see them as special problems and will demand that 'something should be done'. This greater awareness of the crime will mean that more people will report incidents to the police and the police will be more likely to take some action.

In some cases this can create a sense of *moral panic*. The crimes are seen as a threat to the whole of society. Vandalism, football hooliganism and mugging are often at the centre of moral panics.

As well as affecting the reporting of crime, moral panics also make people more aware of certain crimes and can increase their sense of fear that they might become a victim.

The Crime Survey

Another source of evidence on crime is the British Crime Survey. This is a form of social research that is quite separate from the work of the police and the courts. Crime surveys are studies of victims.

The British Crime Survey which started in 1981 is a survey of 16 000 people sampled at random from the electoral registers. Each person is shown a list of offences and asked if they had been the victim of any of these crimes. Those who were victims were then asked to give further details and to say what action had been taken. Finally the survey collected information on people's lifestyle, their contacts with the police and how they felt about crime.

The Crime Surveys have shown that 'dark figure' varies with different crimes. The chance of a crime being reported to the police and of being recorded is higher for some crimes than for others. Only a small number of the cases of vandalism are reported and even fewer are recorded. All thefts involving motor vehicles are reported and all are recorded.

Fear of crime worries many people. Often the fear of being a victim of crime is much greater than the actual chance of becoming a victim.

Many old people are afraid of being mugged on the street. The crime surveys have shown that they are in fact the least likely to become victims of mugging. Young men are the least afraid yet are in reality the most likely to be mugged.

Table 10.1   How safe do you feel walking alone in this area after dark?

	Percentage who felt 'very unsafe'				Percentage who were victims of 'street crime'
	Inner cities	Other city areas	Other areas	All areas	All areas
	%	%	%	%	%
Men aged					
16–30	3	1	1	1	7.7
31–60	11	3	1	4	6.6
60+	27	12	6	7	0.6
Women					
16–30	28	18	11	16	2.8
31–60	38	21	13	35	1.4
60+	60	41	29	37	1.2

(Source: *British Crime Survey 1983*, Home Office Research Study, Tables 4 and 5)

Figure 10·7 Which crime causes most worry?

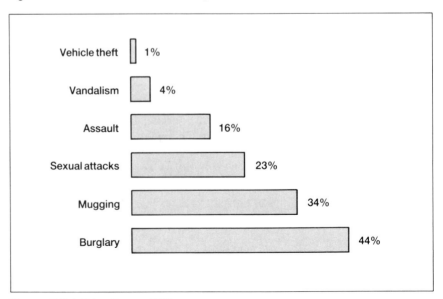

(Source: British Crime Survey, 1981)

Figure 10·8 Levels of recorded and unrecorded crime, 1983

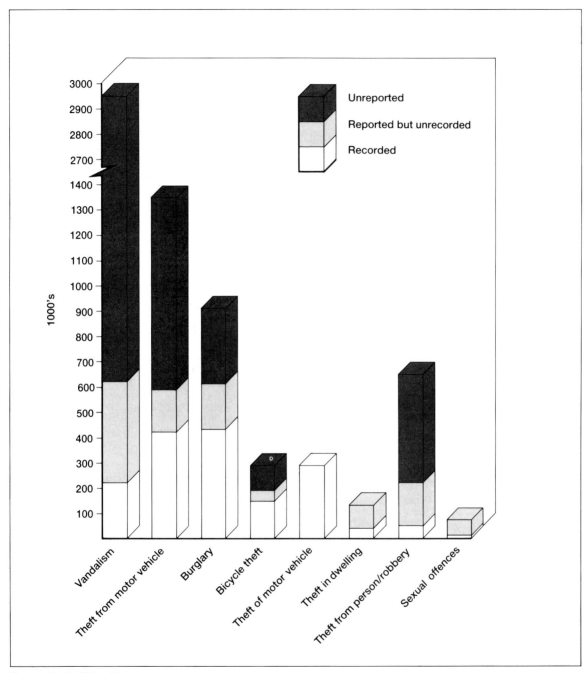

(Source: British Crime Survey)

Questions

1. Why are some crimes not reported to the police?
2. Why might there be a sudden increase in the number of reported cases of vandalism?
3. The 1983 British Crime Survey compared people's fear of going out and their chances of being robbed or attacked. The results are shown in Table 10.1. Which of the following statements are true and which are false?
4. The evidence from the British Crime Survey shows that people who are less afraid of going out at night are more likely to become victims of street crime. How might you explain this?

Figure 10.9

	True	False
a. Men are more likely than women to be victims of street crime		
b. Older men are more likely than younger men to be victims of street crime		
c. Of the elderly women interviewed over half of those who lived in the inner cities felt unsafe on the streets at night		
d. Women feel more unsafe at night and are more likely to be attacked		
e. Older people feel safer going out at night because they are less likely to be victims of crime		
f. Older men are more likely than younger men to feel unsafe when out at night		

10.5   The courts

Anyone who is charged with a crime, will come before a *criminal court*. Other courts, known as *civil courts*, deal with arguments and disputes.

In a criminal court the 'defendant' is prosecuted, usually by the police. In a civil court the defendant is sued by a plaintiff. Some legal problems are so specialised that the ordinary civil courts would have difficulty dealing with them. They are dealt with by special courts, known as *tribunals*. They are similar to courts but only take on one type of case. Another specialised court is the coroners court which deals with cases involving suspicious deaths.

The courts are organised at different levels. The higher courts handle the more serious or difficult cases. Some courts have the power to change the decisions made by other courts. This happens when someone 'appeals' against the verdict that has been reached. The highest court in the United Kingdom is The House of Lords. The decisions of the House of Lords must be followed by all other courts.

The magistrates

For most people who are in trouble the local magistrates' court is their first contact with the law. Magistrates, or Justices of the Peace as they are also known, were introduced by Richard I at the end of the twelfth century. They are still an important part of English law.

Magistrates' courts meet in most towns two or three times a week. It is only in the largest cities that the magistrates are full-time lawyers. Most of the 25 000 magistrates in England and Wales are ordinary people carrying-out their duties, without pay, in their spare time.

Magistrates deal with the less serious criminal cases. These are known as *summary offences*. The more serious, or *indictable offences*, are tried in the crown court unless the defendant pleads guilty and agrees to being dealt with by the magistrate.

As well as dealing with criminal cases the magistrates' courts have special responsibility for cases involving young people. They are also responsible for a number of other matters such as licensing public houses, restaurants and betting shops.

The crown court

Any court case involves two sides. In a criminal case the *prosecution* is usually known as 'The Crown' and tries to prove the charges. Against the prosecution there is the *defence*.

Each side will have its own lawyers and will call its own witnesses. The evidence will be presented for the jury to hear and the witnesses cross-examined. When all has been said the judge will explain any important legal points to the jury and will send them away to consider their verdict. If the verdict is guilty the judge will then pass sentence. An important case involving many witnesses can take many weeks. Having lawyers to defend you in a trial can be very expensive, often costing hundreds of pounds a day. Most people are therefore entitled to *legal aid* which covers the cost of their defence.

Civil courts

Civil courts deal with many different types of dispute. They can grant divorces, sort out claims for damages and settle arguments over the ownership of property. There is no jury. The judge, or in some cases the recorder, hears the evidence and makes the decision. The less important cases are dealt with by county courts. More serious cases go to the High Court. When someone loses a civil case they have to pay damages to the winner.

Figure 10·10 The courts

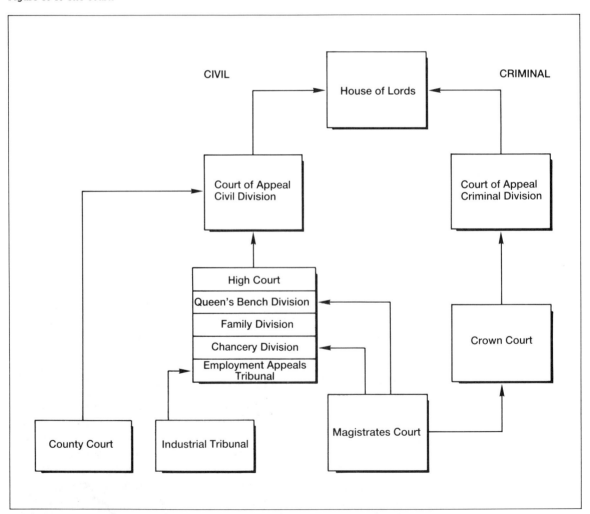

Cases in the civil court may be concerned with broken promises or with *civil wrongs*. A civil wrong happens when you suffer as a result of someone else's actions. You may have been injured as a result of negligence or someone may be causing a nuisance near to your home. You may go to court to sue for damages or to get them to stop.

Solicitors and barristers

Anyone who has a legal problem is likely to go to a solicitor. This could involve the legal side of buying a house, writing a will or just getting advice on matters of law. If a court case is likely the solicitor may act on behalf of the client, presenting the case and answering legal points, or may call in a barrister.

A barrister only deals with court cases. Some barristers specialise in criminal cases, others with divorce or insurance. In a serious case the solicitor will prepare all of the evidence and 'brief' the barrister who will argue the case in court.

Scotland and Northern Ireland

Scotland and Northern Ireland have their own legal systems with their own traditions and customs. In Scotland the police collect the evidence and leave it to the Procurator-fiscal to decide if there is a case to answer.

If British citizens feel unfairly treated by the government or by the law the case can be taken to the European Court of Justice or the European Court of Human Rights. In some cases the European courts have the power to make governments change the country's laws.

Questions

Which courts would deal with the following cases?
1. **a** A man charged with bank robbery
   b An argument between neighbours
   c A divorce
   d A claim for damages arising from an injury at work
   e An inquiry into a suspicious death
   f A young person charged with stealing from a supermarket
2. Find the errors in the following sentences and re-write them correctly.
   a In a civil case the jury hears all of the evidence and then decides on the verdict.
   b In England the police give all of the evidence to the Procurator-fiscal who decides if there is a case to answer.
   c In a civil court the plaintiff is prosecuted by the defence.
   d The defendant in a criminal case is called to give evidence against the witnesses.
   e Juvenile courts deal with cases of suspicious death while the coroner is concerned with accidents at work.
   f A barrister will take on any legal problem from helping you to write your will to defending you in court.

10.6 A serious accident

Figure 10·11 Going to court

CRIMINAL PROCEEDINGS

THE CIVIL CASE

After the accident Jennifer Brown spent many weeks in hospital. She was unable to go back to her old job and still has difficulty in walking. She decides to sue Terry Jones for negligence.

Jennifer goes to see her solicitor who tells her that she has a good chance of getting damages.

The solicitor issues a writ for damages against Terry Jones' insurance company who are liable for any claims which are a result of the accident.

As you are still out of work you should have no problem getting legal aid.

The insurance company ask for a meeting. They offer Jennifer Brown £10 000 to settle out-of-court.

Jennifer is surprised by the amount that was offered. Her solicitor advised her not to settle. She believes that they will get more from the court.

It's a lot of money.

Three years after the accident Jennifer's case has come to court.

Jennifer Brown's barrister calls her as a witness. The defence barrister cross-examines her, trying to find any weakness in her evidence.

Jennifer's barrister makes his closing speach.

. . . and I award you damages of £15,000.

The judge decides that Terry Jones had been negligent and awards Jennifer Brown damages and costs against the insurance company.

10.7   Explaining crime

One way of explaining crime is to see it as a physical, or medical, problem. Crime is thought to be like an illness which infects people in the same way as influenza or chicken-pox. If the criminal is given the right sort of treatment then he or she will be cured. Physical explanations may even see crime as an hereditary disease which is passed on from parents to children. Crime is often linked to some form of mental illness.

Explaining crime in this way is not very satisfactory. Most people who commit crimes are perfectly sane and well. There is nothing to show that they are any different from anyone else. In some cases people have very good reasons for behaving in a criminal way.

A better way to understand crime it to consider it as a social problem. It is linked to the social environment within which people live their lives. At a very simple level this is a matter of saying that someone has not learned how to tell right from wrong. Social scientists would say that the individual has not been properly socialised. Their socialisation did not teach them how to be law-abiding members of society.

The young child may not have experienced the warmth and trust that is an important part of primary socialisation. It could also be that although the child was given warmth and affection within the family it was taught the wrong things. A third approach could be to say that although the child was brought up to respect law and order and to behave in a law-abiding way, later life introduced him or her to criminal ways.

There is an important link between crime and the environment. Some places have far higher levels of crime than others. As long ago as the eighteenth century the cities were seen as places where crime flourished.

In the nineteenth century children who were in trouble with the law would be sent to homes in the countryside. This kept them away from what people saw as the evil effects of city life. Areas of cities which have the highest levels of crime are also the areas of the greatest unemployment, the worst living conditions and the fewest opportunities.

Explaining crime is not only a matter of knowing why people break the law but also why the law is there in the first place. If there were no laws there could be no crime and therefore no criminals. A complete explanation of why there is crime should also examine who makes the laws and why they make them.

Discussion

Which of the following statements explain crime in terms of:
a physical or biological causes?
b socialisation?
c environment?

1. 'They are all criminals from that area, not an honest person among them.'
2. 'What can you expect! No one ever showed him any affection, he was bound to turn out a bad lot.'
3. 'She would never have gone straight. You've only got to look at what happened to her parents. It is in the family.'
4. 'If he could have got away he might have had a chance but not living among that lot of crooks.'
5. 'I always said there was something wrong with him. I think it must have been in the blood.'
6. 'Our policy is to attack the causes of crime by removing the neighbourhoods that are its breeding grounds. We will build new estates on the edge of the city.'

CASE STUDY

Mods and Rockers

A Bank Holiday is a time when everyone likes to have a break and enjoy themselves. For a number of years during the 1960s, Bank Holidays were linked in many people's minds to the problems of Mods and Rockers.

It all started at Clacton on Easter Sunday in 1963. It was a cold wet day and there was not much to do. Gangs of young people chased each other across the beach and onto the streets while youths on motor-bikes roared up and down the promenade. At the end of the day twenty-four young men had been arrested by the police.

On the following day the 'Clacton riots' were front-page news. What had begun as an incident involving a few hundred young people became a national problem.

The events at Clacton and the way they were reported had two important effects. Young people who had little to do on Bank Holidays learned that seaside resorts were the places to go to for fun and excitement. Those concerned with law and order came to believe that young people who rode about on motorbikes or wore a particular type of clothing were troublemakers.

By the next Bank Holiday the seaside resorts were prepared. Extra police were on duty. Shops were boarded up or displayed signs refusing to serve young people. Everyone was on the lookout for the first signs of trouble. Any hint of trouble would lead to arrests.

As a result there were more arrests and the newspapers were able to report 'an increase in seaside violence'. The newspapers did not report that most of the arrests were for very minor offences. Many young people were released without being charged and the cost of the extra precautions was many times that of the damage caused.

The newspaper headlines were enough to increase concerns about hooliganism. New laws were called for. There were demands for magistrates to deal severely with troublemakers. Even more precautions were taken to prevent trouble.

Many causes were given for 'the riots'. Some blamed the parents, others blamed the schools. Some people said that young people had too much money to spend while others blamed it on unemployment and dead-end jobs. The real cause was the way people reacted to the events of each Bank Holiday. Just as an amplifier increases the sound of a record player so the reactions to the events amplified the seriousness of what actually happened.

Discussion

Arrange the following events into the correct order to show how deviance can be amplified.

The press are there to report the trouble as it takes place.
There are calls for tougher action against hooligans.
The newspapers describe it as a riot.
The word gets around that there is going to be trouble and people go along to see what happens.
The police are on the look-out for trouble.
The government considers passing new laws.
The press praises the police for their work but warn people that there is more trouble to come.
A group of young people get into trouble.
Magistrates hand out very stiff sentences.
More young people are arrested.

10.8   Vocabulary

Civil court
A court of law which settles disputes and arguments.

Collator
A police officer who collects and analyses evidence on crime in a local area.

County court
A court which hears the more serious civil cases.

Court of appeal
A court which hears cases 'sent on appeal' from a lower court and reconsiders the evidence.

Crime
Behaviour which breaks the law.

Crown court
A court which tries the more serious criminal cases.

Customs
Behaviour that is governed by tradition as 'the way things have always been done'.

The defence
The lawyers and others who seek to disprove charges brought in a court case.

Defendant
The person who is being tried or sued in a court case.

Deviance
Behaviour which goes against the accepted behaviour of a particular group.

Etiquette
Rules for the correct behaviour in a social situation, for example when meeting someone, at a party or at a meal.

Fashion
Informal rules about dress and appearance which change very often.

Formal rules
Rules that are written down in a rule book.

Indictable offences
More serious criminal offences which are dealt with by the crown courts.

Informal rules
Rules that are generally accepted by those concerned but are not written down.

Home beat officer
A police officer who only works in one small district which he or she looks after and gets to know.

Norms
Expectations of the behaviour appropriate to any situation.

Paramilitary
Any civilian group which has the characteristics of the army.

Plaintiff
The person who brings an action in a civil court.

Procurator-fiscal
An official in the Scottish legal system.

The prosecution
The police and lawyers who seek to prove charges against the defendant in a court case.

Summary offences
Minor offences dealt with by the magistrates court.

CHAPTER 11   INEQUALITY AND POVERTY

People differ in many ways. Some may be taller, or stronger, or more athletic than others. No two people are ever exactly the same. They may have differences of taste or fashion. One person may prefer wholemeal bread while someone else only eats white. One may wear bright clothes and like classical music while the other prefers darker colours and listens to pop.

Differences can mean that some people have an advantage over others. They may be better footballers, better dancers or better artists. When they are placed alongside one another it is clear that they are not equal. Differences in talent and skill are quite normal. You would not expect everyone to be equally good at everything.

Individuals can be unequal in other ways. One person may have more opportunities to develop their skills. Others may own more or be paid more. They may have more power to do things and to influence what others do. At times the differences between those who have and those who don't can be very great. You may even consider that such inequalities are not fair, that there is a lack of justice in some having more than others. Such inequalities occur in every society and give rise to the same questions of fairness and social justice.

UNIVERSAL DECLARATION OF HUMAN RIGHTS

WHEREAS *recognition of the inherent dignity and of the equal and inalienable rights of all members of the human family is the foundation of freedom, justice and peace in the world,*

WHEREAS *disregard and contempt for human rights have resulted in barbarous acts which have outraged the conscience of mankind, and the advent of a world in which human beings shall enjoy freedom of speech and belief and*

Article 1. All human beings are born free and equal in dignity and rights. They are endowed with reason and conscience and should act towards one another in a spirit of brotherhood.

Article 2. Everyone is entitled to all the rights and freedoms set forth in this Declaration, without distinction of any kind, such as race, colour, sex, language, religion, political or other opinion, national or social origin, property, birth or other status.

Furthermore, no distinction shall be made on the basis of the political, jurisdictional or international status of the country or territory to which a person belongs, whether it be independent, trust, non-self-governing or under any other limitation of sovereignty.

Article 3. Everyone has the right to life, liberty and security of person.

Article 4. No one shall be held in slavery or servitude; slavery and the slave trade shall be prohibited in all their forms.

Article 5. No one shall be subjected to torture or to cruel, inhuman or degrading treatment or punishment.

Article 6. Everyone has the right to recognition everywhere as a person before the law.

Article 7. All are equal before the law and are entitled without any discrimination to equal protection of the law. All are entitled to equal protection against any discrimination in violation of this Declaration and against any incitement to such discrimination.

Article 20. (1) Everyone has the right to freedom of peaceful assembly and association.

(2) No one may be compelled to belong to an association.

Article 21. (1) Everyone has the right to take part in the government of his country, directly or through freely chosen representatives.

(2) Everyone has the right of equal access to public service in his country.

(3) The will of the people shall be the basis of the authority of government; this will shall be expressed in periodic and genuine elections which shall be by universal and equal suffrage and shall be held by secret vote or by equivalent free voting procedures.

Article 22. Everyone, as a member of society, has the right to social security and is entitled to realization, through national effort and international co-operation and in accordance with the organization and resources of each State, of the economic, social and cultural rights indispensable for his dignity and the free development of his personality.

Article 23. (1) Everyone has the right to work, to free choice of employment, to just and favourable conditions of work and to protection against unemployment.

(2) Everyone, without any discrimination, has the right to equal pay for equal work.

(3) Everyone who works has the right to just and favourable re-

11.1   Wealth and income

Inequality often arises from the ways in which resources are shared out. Wealth and income are not distributed equally across the whole of society. To understand this inequality we need to know how wealth and income are produced. What has been the effect of the state's attempts to gain a more equal distribution?

Wealth

Wealth is what you own. Someone who is wealthy owns a great deal. Someone who is poor owns very little. The most wealthy in society have their wealth in property and investments. This wealth gives them an income and produces even more wealth. Wealth is not shared out evenly amongst the whole population. A small number of people own most of the wealth. In the early part of this century 1% of the population owned over 60% of the wealth.

Some families have been able to build up very large amounts of wealth by handing it down from generation to generation over many centuries. For the past sixty years there have been taxes on wealth. *Capital transfer taxes* must be paid when wealth is handed on. These 'death duties' are paid when someone who owns a certain amount of wealth dies.

Table 11.1   Distribution of wealth, 1971–1983

Percentage of wealthy	Share of total wealth		
	1971 %	1979 %	1983 %
Top 1%	31	22	20
Top 5%	52	40	40
Top 10%	65	54	54
Top 25%	86	77	77
Top 50%	97	96	96

(Source: adapted from *Social Trends*, 1986, Table 5.22, HMSO)

Taxes on wealth have had the greatest effect on the very, very wealthy. Some of their wealth has been shared out among the very wealthy and the fairly wealthy. There is no evidence that taxes on wealth have done much to help people who are not at all wealthy.

In 1983 the top 1% owned 20% of the wealth. The most wealthy quarter of the population owned three-quarters of the wealth. The least wealthy half shared only 4% of the wealth between them.

Not all wealth is made up of country estates and yachts on the French Riviera. For most people their only wealth is the house that they live in and the money they are saving for their pension. When these forms of wealth are included in the total we still find that half of the population own four-fifths of the wealth.

Income

People receive their income in many different ways. They may receive it in their wage packet at the end of the week or as a monthly salary cheque. Many people rely on the state for their income in the form of social security or unemployment benefit. Income can also come from wealth. Money in the bank earns interest. Investments in shares give dividends. Property produces rent. There are great differences between the incomes of the highest and the lowest paid.

In 1984 the average weekly wage for manual workers was £143. Those who worked in the lowest paid manual jobs earned a little over £100. Non-manual workers did slightly better earning an average of £172 a week.

In the same year the best paid company director in Britain earned £14 838 each week. He and 337 other 'top people' earned an average of nearly £3000 each week, or twenty-times the weekly wage of the average manual worker.

Many of those with the highest earnings only receive a small part of their income from the job that they do. Many also hold shares in the firms that they run. When the company profits are added to the salary from the job some company bosses can earn more than £1 000 000 a year.

Figure 11·1

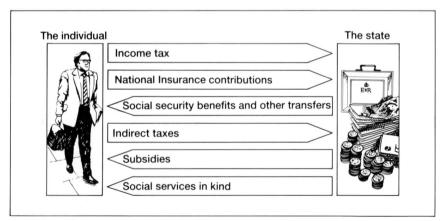

Taxes and benefits

Just as capital transfer tax is a way of reducing inequalities of wealth,

Figure 11·2 The rate for the job. Weekly earnings (1984) before tax

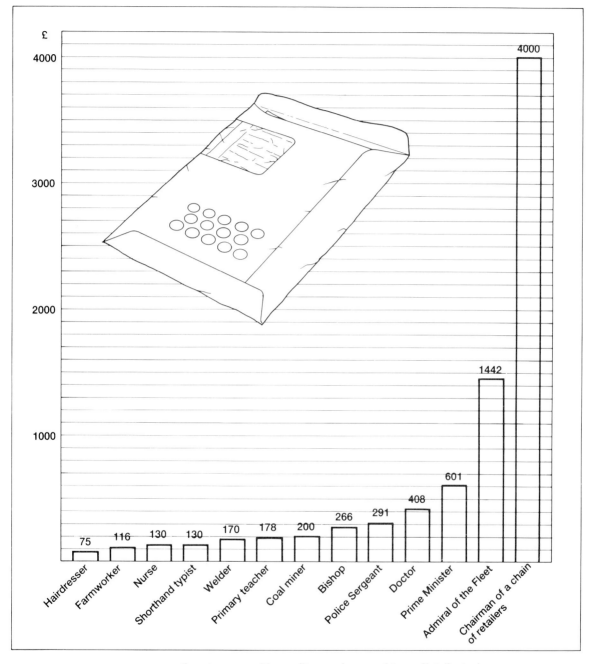

so other taxes and benefits can be used to redistribute income.

Those with the highest incomes pay a greater proportion of their earnings to the government in tax. They not only pay a higher rate of income tax but will pay more in indirect taxes. Those on low incomes pay very little tax and often none at all. They are also more likely to use state benefits. The rich also receive state benefits. Their children may go to state schools, they may use the National Health Service. Along with everyone else they will receive certain 'universal' benefits like retirement pensions when they are 65. Benefits may either be in cash or in services.

When a family receives more in benefits than it pays out in tax it will be better off. If it pays more tax it will be worse off. Those families on the highest incomes pay out much more than they receive.

Table 11.2   Redistributing income

	Annual income of families with:		
	Lowest incomes	Middle incomes	Highest incomes
	1	2	3
	£	£	£
Income	120	6880	18640
+			
Cash benefits	3020	1100	600
−			
Income tax and National Insurance	10	1410	4510
−			
Indirect taxes	850	1860	3380
+			
Value of services	1340	1470	1560
=			
Disposable income	3620	6180	12910
Gains and losses	+3500	− 700	−5730

(Source: adapted from *Social Trends*, 1986, Table 5.19, HMSO)

Questions
1. Give three examples of things that could be counted as wealth.
2. Give three examples of things that could be counted as income.
3. What percentage of the nation's wealth was owned by the top 10% of wealth-owners in 1971? How far had this changed by 1983?
4. By how much did the percentage of the nation's wealth owned by the bottom 50% of wealth-owners rise between 1971 and 1983?
5. Would a family on the lowest income gain or lose from the redistribution of taxes and benefits? Explain why.

11.2   Poverty

What do we mean when we say that someone is poor?

Do we mean that they have nothing at all, that they only just have enough to live on, or that they have less than others?

Many people in drought-stricken areas of the world where there is not enough food are clearly in poverty. Many die because they do not have enough to eat. Few people die of starvation in Britain. Does this mean that people in Britain cannot be in poverty?

Absolute and relative poverty

Many people in the poorer regions of the world are living in *absolute poverty*. They do not have enough food to maintain the lowest level of subsistence. Absolute poverty is often regarded as the minimum food, clothes and shelter that people need if they are able to survive. When you consider the levels of starvation in many areas of Africa it is difficult to imagine anyone being in absolute poverty in Britain. Yet many people would say that they are poor.

Instead of seeing poverty as lacking the minimum food, clothing and shelter needed for survival we could regard it as being without those

things that most people take for granted. This is a *relative* view of poverty because it relates poverty to the way-of-life of the majority of people. If it is generally believed that everyone should have a refrigerator, an inside toilet and a television then those who don't have them are in poverty.

Figure 11·3 The rise in poverty, 1979–83

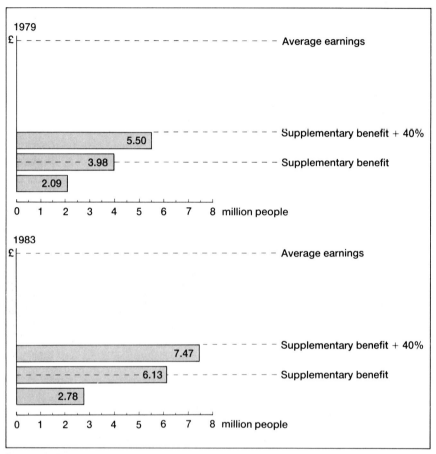

Source: CPAG

The poverty line

If we are to know who is in poverty we need to be able to decide where to draw the *poverty line*. This is the level of income below which families are in poverty.

To draw the line for absolute poverty means deciding what a family needs. This means finding out the minimum that people need if they are to survive. This could be called the *subsistence level*. Deciding the level for relative poverty is more difficult. It involves making decisions on the minimum standard of living that people would accept.

If it is to be useful in measuring poverty the 'poverty line' needs to clear and easy to use. The state has a level of income below which families can claim *income support*, or supplementary benefit. This can be used as a 'poverty line'. This is the state's standard of poverty. In Britain the state's poverty line is an absolute standard linked to a subsistence standard of living. It does not tell us anything about relative poverty.

Another way of drawing a 'poverty line' would be to link it to the average level of incomes. Those in poverty could then be those on the bottom 10% of incomes or those who receive less than half of average earnings. This is known as a *relative income* approach because it relates poverty to incomes. Although it is a way of measuring relative poverty it can be misleading. Incomes could rise and everyone could be much better off. There would still be a bottom 10% who on this method would still be in poverty.

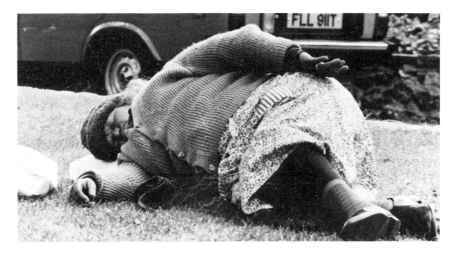

Relative deprivation

Neither the state's minimum standard nor the relative income approach take account of what people think it means to be poor. People may be poor on the state's poverty line and may be in the bottom income groups but, when asked, may not think themselves to be poor at all. They can only compare themselves with those around them, many of whom are likely to be in a similar situation. Relative to those they meet every day they may be quite well off. They would not see themselves as deprived in any way. Deprivation is relative to what you see around you.

Peter Townsend in his enquiry into 'Poverty in the United Kingdom' constructed a *relative deprivation* index. He began with a list of 60 activities. The interviewers asked people if they had a cooked breakfast on most days of the week and if they owned a refrigerator; had they had a holiday away from home in the last 12 months or been out for a meal in the past fortnight? The answers showed how the lifestyles of different groups of people varied. They could be compared to incomes to give a measure of relative deprivation.

Townsend's research showed that the state's poverty line was a long way below the income which the majority of people thought was poverty. Someone would still be considered poor if they had an income which was half as much again as the state provided under income support, or supplementary benefit.

Project: Breadline Britain

In 1983 London Weekend Television carried out a follow-up to Townsend's study. They asked a sample of people what they thought was necessary for a minimum standard of living. Some of the results are shown in Figure 11.4.

Use the 'Breadline Britain' list to carry out your own survey of what people think is meant by poverty. How far do your results fit the view that poverty is relative?

Figure 11·4

Percentage of people who describe each item as necessary	
Heating to warm the home	97%
Indoor toilet, not shared	96%
Damp-free home	96%
Bath, not shared with another household	94%
Two pairs of all-weather shoes	78%
Refrigerator	77%
Toys for children	71%
Carpets in living room and bedrooms	70%
Meat or fish every other day	63%
A television	51%
A 'best outfit' for special occasions	48%
A dressing gown	36%
A night out once a fortnight	28%

(Source: adapted from *Poor Britain* by J. Mack and S. Lansley, George Allen and Unwin, 1985)

11.3   Who is in poverty?

In 1983 one-third of the population of Britain lived in poverty. Many more people had lived in poverty at some point in their lives. Families with low incomes move in and out of poverty. The effects of poverty change as the family changes. There is a cycle of poverty which follows the cycle of people's lives.

Bringing-up children can be a time of hardship for a family with a low income. In time the children will grow up, leave school and find jobs. If there is no work they will go on to 'the dole'. For a while the family has a number of bread-winners and may be quite well off. They move out of poverty. In time the grown-up children will marry and move away. The parents will be left alone. As long as they are working they will be quite comfortable.

Figure 11·5 The bottom 20% of incomes

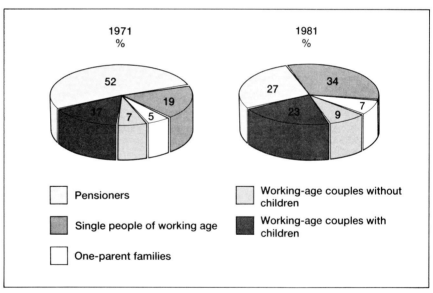

(Source: Social Trends, 1986, Chart 5·17)

The married children will not be too badly off either. Until they start families of their own they will have the advantage of two pay-packets. There may be money to spare for holidays in the sun and even for a small car. As the parents get older they must face a new problem. Retirement brings a drop in income and they find that they cannot live as cheaply as they did. They get colder and need to spend more on heating. They may be ill and need extra help. In retirement they could easily cross the line back into poverty.

Their children may now have children of their own. The wife may have to give up her job. The family income is reduced just at the time that life becomes more expensive. Starting a family means extra food, clothes, presents at Christmas and birthdays and many other new expenses. At this time of their lives they may well move back into poverty again. And so the cycle continues . . . .

Who are the poor?

Low incomes are an important cause of poverty. The largest group of people who are living on low incomes are single people of working age. They may be unemployed or working in very low paid jobs.

An increasing number of old people end their lives in residential homes or hostels.

Figure 11·6 The welfare state

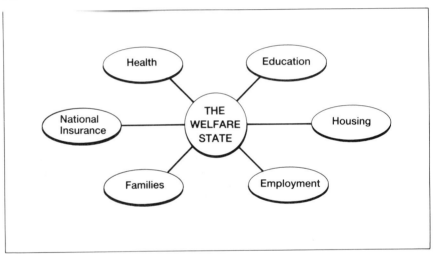

A family's income can be low for many reasons. Many workers receive very low pay. In 1981 680 000 people with full-time jobs earned less than the level of supplementary benefit. In unskilled jobs, wages, particularly for women, can be too low to support a family. It is often necessary for both husband and wife to work long hours if they are to earn enough money for their family's needs. Nearly a quarter of those on low incomes have families with young children.

The difficulties faced by single-parents are even greater than those faced by two-parent families. Most single parents are women. Many must bring up their children on state benefits. If they can find work it is likely to be the lowest paid work of all.

The unemployed also have to live on low incomes. They frequently depend on income support. Unemployment benefit is not generous. It is intended to be less than might be earned by working in the lowest paid jobs.

Old people also depend on the state for their income. Pensions are often inadequate and the elderly are forced to seek extra help from income support, or supplementary benefit. Many old people who could get extra help do not ask for it. They prefer to keep their independence and not to take what they see as charity. In 1985 one in three old age pensioners who were entitled to supplementary benefit did not claim it.

Families with young children are more likely to be poor than those without children. Large families are even more likely to be in poverty. Families that survive on low incomes are not just short of money. They lose out in other ways as well. Housing conditions are worse. Children have to share bedrooms. Homes are often damp and may be without bathrooms or toilets. The family's health suffers. Infant mortality is higher. Children do less well at school and seldom undertake training after they leave school. Even the expectation of life is less for those in poverty.

Table 11.3 Percentage of full-time employees earning less than £100 per week, 1984

	Men %	Women %
North of England	11.2	17.9
Yorkshire and Humberside	11.9	18.4
North-West of England	11.3	15.9
East Midlands	12.0	20.9
West Midlands	10.9	17.3
East Anglia	13.1	16.2
South-East of England	7.8	8.9
South-West of England	13.4	18.3
Great Britain	10.5	14.5

(Source: adapted from *Regional Trends*, 1985, Tables 8.7 and 8.8, HMSO)

Questions
The proportion of people on low incomes varies between different parts of the country.

1. What percentage of men and women in Great Britain earned less than £100 a week in 1984?
2. In which region was the percentage of men earning less than £100 a week less than the figure for Great Britain as a whole?
3. In which region was the difference between the percentage of low-paid men and of low-paid women greatest?
4. Does the table support the view that the south of England is more prosperous than the north?

11.4   The beginnings of the welfare state

In the middle of the nineteenth century the middle and upper classes knew little about the lives of the poor. They seldom ventured away from the main streets of the cities into the back alleys and slums where the poorest people lived. It was left to writers like Charles Dickens and Benjamin Disraeli to present a picture of the poverty through their novels.

Those in need depended on local 'Boards of Guardians' or on charity. For many, poverty meant the workhouses and a *pauper's* grave. By paying a few pence each week into a Friendly Society people could gain some protection against illness, unemployment and old age. Many people could not even afford that.

The early poverty studies

In 1885 the *Pall Mall Gazette* published a survey which claimed that one in every four Londoners lived in poverty. Charles Booth knew the East End of London well and considered the report to be exaggerated. He set out to conduct his own survey to prove the newspaper wrong. He began a massive enquiry into the conditions of the poor in London. Information was collected from the School Board visitors who knew every street and every family with young children. To this he added evidence from the Poor Law and the police.

The Whitechapel district of London in 1870.

After three years Booth had completed the first part of his enquiry. Booth's evidence showed that the newspapers had not exaggerated. They had underestimated the amount of poverty. One-third of the people in the East End were living in poverty. His research was the first real attempt to carry out a large-scale social survey of poverty.

Booth's work in London set an example which was soon followed by Seebohm Rowntree in York. His studies were carried out in 1899, 1936 and 1950. With the help of doctors he drew up a minimum shopping list of the food needed to sustain a family of four. The cost of this shopping basket became his poverty line.

The evidence collected by Booth and Rowntree made it clear that something had to be done about the conditions of the poor. Between 1906 and 1911 the Liberal government introduced old age pensions, school meals and the first schemes of national health and unemployment insurance.

The years between the two World Wars were a time of high unemployment and even greater poverty. In 1932, 23% of the labour force were unemployed. The National Insurance scheme was stretched to its limit. It was not until 1942, in the middle of the Second World War, that Sir William Beveridge proposed a system of welfare and national insurance which would provide for people's needs 'from the cradle to the grave'. Beveridge called for an attack on the five 'giants' of disease, ignorance, squalor, idleness and want.

Sir William Beveridge in 1942.

The welfare state

The post-war Labour government acted on Beveridge's ideas. The National Insurance Act and the National Health Service Act came into effect in 1948. They were an important part of what came to be called the *welfare state*.

It was not a completely new approach to poverty. Many of the ideas could be traced back to the early years of the century. Beveridge combined the various parts together into a single scheme which applied equally to everyone. The cost was to be covered by contributions paid by all of those in work, by employers and by the government.

The National Health Service aimed to provide free health care for everyone. This included hospitals, clinics, doctors and dentists. The National Insurance Act extended the 1911 insurance scheme to cover everyone. It provided insurance against unemployment, sickness and disability as well as maternity benefits and pensions on retirement. Families received support in a number of ways. Mothers received maternity grants as well as child benefit.

'Education for all' was introduced in 1944. It was free and compulsory. Parents on low incomes could receive help with school uniform, travel and school meals. Grants were available to make it possible for all who gained the right qualifications to go on to college and university.

Figure 11.7

THE PHILANTHROPIC HIGHWAYMAN.
Mr. Lloyd-George. "I'LL MAKE 'EM PITY THE AGED POOR!"

(Source: *Punch*, 5 August 1908)

Local welfare services

The system of state benefits and health care is only one part of the whole pattern of social welfare which developed after the Second World War.

Many of the personal social services are provided by local councils which have replaced the Boards of Guardians. Local authorities provide child welfare clinics, help for the homeless, homes for children and the elderly, meals-on-wheels, home helps and day centres. Social workers are employed to look after those in greatest need.

The shortage of homes between the wars had led many councils to build council houses. After the Second World War the government provided grants and laid down regulations about housing standards and rents. Town planning was introduced to control the spread of towns and to prevent the growth of new slums.

Questions
1. Why did Charles Booth begin his survey?
2. Where did Booth get his evidence from?
3. The result of the survey of East London was not expected. Why?
4. Who else carried out surveys of the poor at the end of the last century?
5. What action was taken as a result of these surveys?
6. In what ways did Beveridge's ideas provide help 'from the cradle to the grave'?

11.5   The elderly

There are over ten million pensioners in Britain. They make up nearly 15% of the total population. An increasing number of the elderly are aged 75 or over.

In 1870 men could expect to live, on average, until the age of 41 and women until 45. By the 1980s the expectation of life for women had risen to 74 and for men to 69. People are living longer than they did a century ago. This is a result of improved standards of living and better health. Today men and women expect to have a long period of retirement when their working lives have finished. People are retiring younger.

Women, on average, live longer than men. There are more women over the age of 85 than there are men. At the age of 65 women are twice as likely as men to be widowed. Three-quarters of all women aged over 85 are widows. Many of these old people live alone.

The elderly are not very different from the rest of society. People do not suddenly change when they pass the age of 65. For many retirement is an opportunity to do things that there has not been time to do before. Retirement can also be a time when there is less money to do just those things. In 1981 over half of single pensioners and two-fifths of married couples depended on social security and state pensions for up to 90% of their income. Many pensioners have such low incomes that they must rely on supplementary benefit.

The cost-of-living is higher for the elderly than for the rest of society. They need to keep warm and to have a proper diet. Pensioners spend twice as much as the rest of the population on fuel. Their homes are less likely to be properly insulated. Many old people live in poor housing and are without basic amenities. Old people are more likely to be without an inside toilet or a bath.

Old age is a time when many people live in poverty. Those who are most likely to be poor in old age are those who have been on the edge of poverty throughout their lives. The wages of many manual workers only just provided enough for them to live on. They would have found

Pensioners protesting for an increase in the state old-age pension.

it difficult to save much for their retirement. Non-manual workers whose jobs included some form of pension scheme are more likely to live comfortably when they finish work. The large numbers of elderly people who rely on state benefits are in poverty by any standard.

The elderly make their own special demands on the welfare state. They value their independence but as they get older they often find it less easy to do things for themselves. Moving around may become difficult. Old bones are brittle and a slight fall can cause a fracture. Going shopping in icy weather creates extra risks. The elderly need to keep warm. In winter becoming too cold can lead to hypothermia. Old people die from the cold.

Much can be done to make life better for the elderly. Meals-on-wheels services and home helps who come in to help with the cleaning can make all the difference. They also provide a point of contact for someone living on their own. Lunch clubs and social centres provide a place

Figure 11·8 Changes in the elderly population 1951–2001

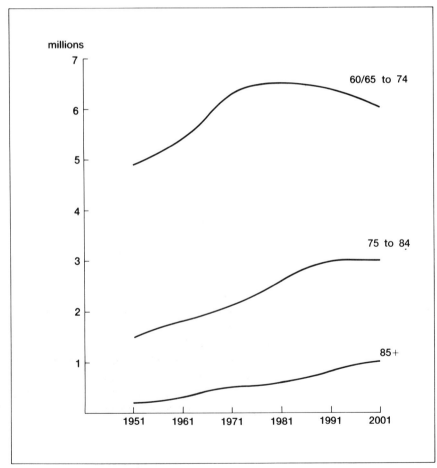

(Source: OPCS, Census Guide 1)

where the elderly can meet. For those who want to stay independent but who sometimes need help there is housing with a warden who is available in an emergency.

Many of the elderly depend on their families. Some may live with their sons or daughters, often within the extended family. Some live nearby. Looking after an elderly person can create its own pressures, making life difficult. Modern houses seldom have the space for an elderly grandparent. A single person may have a job and a career to consider as well as an infirm parent.

Project: facilities for the elderly

Carry out an enquiry into the facilities for the elderly in your area.

You will need to identify the most useful sources of information and decide how you are going to collect it. You may wish to use the public library or the local social services. If you have easy access to old people

Table 11.4 Households with amenities

	Households with elderly persons %	Households without elderly persons %
No bath and no inside toilet	2.5	1.3
No inside toilet	4.4	2.5

(Source: 1981 Census, OPCS)

you could design a questionnaire and conduct interviews. Use the information in the case study of the elderly as a background to your local study. When you have collected and analysed all of the evidence you should write it up as a report or as an exhibition.

You may wish to consider some of the following questions:

What facilities are there for the elderly?
Who provides services for the elderly: the local council, health authorities, voluntary bodies, the elderly themselves or their families?
How far do older people participate in activities provided for the wider population (e.g. adult education classes, libraries, sports facilities, public houses etc.)?
What difficulties do old people and their families face?
What could be done to improve facilities for older people?

11.6   The welfare state today

The welfare state today looks very different from the system proposed by Sir William Beveridge in 1942.

The money needed to provide the welfare state has become far greater than Beveridge anticipated. Rising unemployment and an ageing population have created far greater demands. People expect more than they did fifty years ago. New fields of medicine which were not even imagined in the 1940s have developed. Heart transplants, hip replacements, kidney machines, and body scanners were unknown when the National Health Service was established.

The growth of private medicine

As the pressures on the National Health Service increased, more and more people began to look for other forms of health care. Many chose to get their treatment as private patients.

An operation under way in a modern hospital.

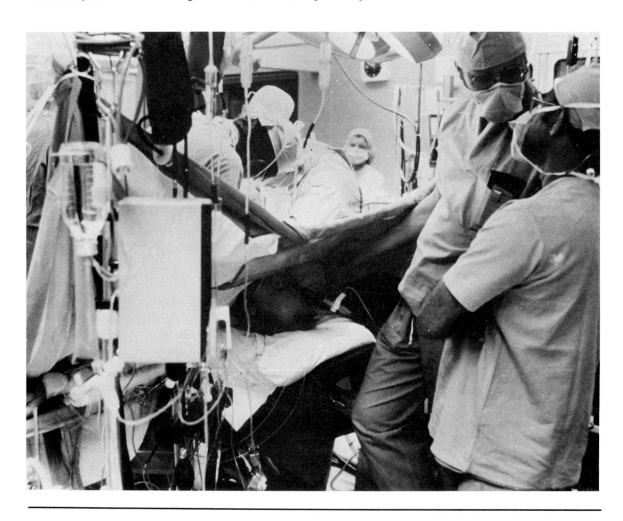

Private schemes cost money. Those who cannot afford to pay for themselves may have medical insurance paid for by their employer. Many employers provide their own welfare services for their staff with everything from factory nurseries to hospital treatment and social facilities.

This has led to the development of a two-tier health service with those who can afford it, or who have medical insurance, paying for private treatment while the rest depend on the state.

The welfare bureaucracy

The job of running the welfare state is shared between a large number of government departments, local councils, regional hospital boards, voluntary societies and many other bodies. In 1981 The Department of Health and Social Security, or DHSS, alone employed 100 000 people.

People often complain that the welfare state is impersonal and bureaucratic. Instead of making things easy, government departments often seem to be making them more difficult. The DHSS make payments according to a complex set of rules which say who is eligible and on what conditions. To make a claim for benefit often involves filling in forms and long waits at the DHSS office.

Stigma

For many people, particularly the elderly, social security is seen as a form of charity and a sign that they can no longer care for themselves. There is a stigma attached to receiving help and many people fail to claim benefits to which they are entitled. Each year hundreds of millions of pounds worth of benefits are not claimed. Even the government only expects three out of every five families that are eligible for 'family credits' to actually claim them.

The poverty trap

This 'poverty trap' arises from the way benefits are paid. Most benefits are 'means tested'. Only when your means fall below a certain level are you able to receive these benefits. If your income increases, you will lose them. A small increase in your means can lead to a large drop in your benefits. Taking a part-time job which brings in £20 a week could lose you benefits worth £25. You are better off not taking the job.

Welfare scroungers

The fear that claimants might be receiving money to which they are not entitled creates a continual pressure against 'welfare scroungers'. In a 1983 survey 63% of those interviewed thought that most supplementary benefit claimants were 'on the fiddle'. Newspaper campaigns against 'benefits fiddles' have often been based on isolated cases. They have had the effect of increasing the sense of stigma in claiming welfare benefits. Social security frauds lose the taxpayer a small fraction of that lost by tax evasion.

The state and welfare

There are two main points-of-view about the role the state should play in the welfare of individuals.

On the one hand there are those who argue that the state should be responsible for the well-being of all citizens. This can best be done by a *universal* welfare scheme. No one is left out and all needs are provided for. This is the view supported by the Labour Party.

The other view is that health, welfare, employment and unemployment are matters for the individual. The state should only provide a 'safety net' for those who are in greatest need. Everyone else should make their own arrangements for insurance and medical care. The 'means test' would determine who needed help. State welfare would be *selective*. Most people should use private schemes. This is the approach taken by the Conservatives.

Questions

1. In what ways has the welfare state changed since Sir William Beveridge produced his report?
2. Why do people choose to pay for their health care? In what ways is paying for health care made easier?
3. Why is the welfare state sometimes described as 'bureaucratic'?
4. Poor families can become trapped in poverty by the system of state benefits. Explain what is meant by the 'poverty trap'.
5. Read the following statements and decide whether they are typical of a 'universal' or of a 'selective' approach to welfare.

Figure 11.9

	Universal approach	A selective approach
It is the duty of the state to provide for all equally		
The state should only provide a 'safety net' for those in greatest need		
The 'means test' is a poor way of providing help for the majority of people		
Individuals should take care of themselves. They should not be allowed to become dependent on the state		
Everyone should have a right to a good standard of health care. There should not be a first-class and a second-class health service		

11.7   Voluntary agencies

In the nineteenth century many of the poor depended on charity. People gave money to provide food, clothing and shelter for those in need. Wealthy individuals built schools for poor children and homes for the elderly. In the poorest districts of the cities charitable societies provided soup kitchens and medical help.

When the state began to provide the health and welfare services it was expected that the voluntary groups would disappear. This did not happen. Today the voluntary agencies are more important than they have ever been. They fill the gaps in the welfare state by helping those who are not provided for and by pioneering new approaches. Many voluntary groups take a more political role, putting pressure on the government to provide more help. Voluntary bodies also provide information and advice both for the government and for those in need. Research into social or medical problems is another important role for the voluntary agencies.

Voluntary organisations are usually charities. They are outside of the state system of welfare and rely for their money on donations and fund-raising. They do not aim to make a profit, unlike many private organisations which run health services and residential homes as businesses. Some voluntary groups are run on a self-help basis.

Participation

Although these groups are 'voluntary' they are not always organised by volunteers. Many of the larger and better known groups have full-time paid workers who run the organisation. There are also many volunteers who help, often in local groups. Voluntary groups make it possible for ordinary people to participate in helping others. They also participate in the work of the welfare state by providing facilities, such as schools and homes, for the state and local agencies to use.

CASE STUDY

Chiswick Women's Aid

In 1971 a number of women in Chiswick got together to protest about rising food prices. As a result of the protest they came into contact with many young mothers who felt lonely and isolated. It was decided to set up a community centre for the women and their children. The local council provided a condemned house and Chiswick Women's Aid began.

Although it was set up as a community centre for young mothers, Chiswick Women's Aid found that more and more women were coming with their children to escape from violent husbands. The house became a refuge for battered women and drew attention to the problem of family violence.

Soon other groups were formed and refuges for women sprang up in many parts of the country. The National Women's Aid Federation (NWAF) was set up to co-ordinate the work of all of the local groups.

Supporters campaign to keep the women's refuge from being closed by the local council.

The attention that was being given to the problems of battered women led to a House of Commons inquiry and then to a White Paper. The government gave grants to NWAF and many local councils helped their local groups. Violence against women in the home became a national issue.

CASE STUDY

Citizens Advice Bureau

There are over 800 Citizen's Advice Bureaus (CAB) in Britain. They are to be found in every town and city.

The CABs form a national organisation which relies on voluntary help. They are independent of both local and political government. Their job is to give advice to anyone who asks for it. You can go into your local CAB and ask for anything from the location of a local youth club to how to take a case to court. Legal problems concern the majority of people who go to the CAB for help. Many of the CABs employ qualified lawyers or would have times when a lawyer is available.

The advice workers who run the local bureaus are all volunteers. They are only allowed to give advice to the public after a period of training. They must work hard to keep up to date. As well as giving advice the

CAB will also help in filling-in forms and with writing letters. When a problem needs expert advice the advice worker will arrange a meeting with someone who specialises in particular problems.

Child Poverty Action Group

CPAG works from the top floor of a dingy building in central London. Squeeze past the duplicator and the photocopying machine and you are in a narrow corridor. Along one side are shelves overflowing with booklets and pamphlets, press releases and campaign newsletters. The focus of CPAG's work is on collection, organising and communicating information.

Since it began in 1965 CPAG has been researching into poverty. Much of its information comes from government sources which is used to support a series of campaigns which have a great influence on the way the government has dealt with poverty.

Discussion

Voluntary agencies perform many different roles. Which roles are performed by the following groups?

Which other voluntary groups do you know about? Which roles do they perform?

Figure 11.10

	Chiswick Women's Aid	Citizens Advice Bureaux	Child Poverty Group
Information and advice to those in need			
Pioneering ways of dealing with new social and welfare problems			
Acting as a pressure group to get things done			
Providing services not included in the welfare state			
Providing an opportunity for people to participate voluntarily in something which is valued			
Providing a way people in need can help themselves			
Co-ordinating the work of a number of voluntary groups			

11.8 Vocabulary

Absolute poverty

Absolute poverty occurs when someone is living below the level of subsistence.

Capital transfer tax

A tax paid on inherited wealth, sometimes known as 'death duties'.

Charity

Giving charity means giving to a good cause. A charity is an organisation which relies for most of its income on voluntary donations and it does not seek to make a profit from its activities.

Death duties

Another name for capital transfer tax.

Dole

An everyday term for unemployment benefit.

Health insurance

All wage-earners pay National Health Insurance out of their wage packets. People may choose to take out private health insurance to cover the cost of private medical treatment.

Income support

The system of social security payments introduced in 1986 which replaced supplementary benefit.

National Insurance

The system of insurance introduced in 1947 to cover the cost of the welfare benefits from regular payments by those in work. It includes National Health Insurance.

Pauper

An old word for someone who is poor.

Poverty line

The level of income below which people fall into poverty.

Poverty trap

A problem which occurs as a result of means-testing benefits and which discourages those on benefits from taking low-paid jobs.

Primary poverty

A term used by Seebohm Rowntree to describe people who were below the poverty line through no fault of their own.

Relative deprivation

The belief that you are worse off in comparison to others.

Relative poverty

A poverty line which is determined in relation to the average level of incomes.

Secondary poverty

A term used by Seebohm Rowntree to describe people who were in poverty because they could not manage what money they had properly.

Social security

The system of welfare benefits developed within the welfare state and which includes family benefits, income support, disability benefits etc.

Subsistence

The minimum standard of living needed to just keep alive.

Supplementary benefit

Social security payments made to people in the greatest need. Now replaced by income support.

CHAPTER 12

MASS COMMUNICATION

Smash!

A brick comes hurtling through your front window! Around the brick is a piece of paper on which is written a message. Is it a sign that someone is trying to tell you something?

The brick, the paper and the writing on it are the medium for delivering the message.

Sending messages by brick is a rather drastic, if not dangerous way of telling someone something. Most messages come to us in much simpler ways. Writing a letter or making a telephone call are better ways of sending a message. You could 'say it with flowers', send a 'kissogram' or hire an aeroplane to tow your message across the sky.

Each of these is a different medium for sending your message. The message could be the same but the medium would be different. The medium is the method used to carry the message. It is the way we communicate messages. When there is more than one medium for carrying messages we describe them as media, and sometimes as 'communications media'.

Any communication involves a message and a medium which carries the message. Sometimes we get the message from the medium itself. A brick through the window tells you quite a lot without reading what is on the paper. The same message sent by kissogram can mean something quite different. When messages are sent to very large numbers of people at the same time using some form of technology, we would describe it as mass media or mass communication.

12.1   Communication

When a message is communicated there must be a *sender* and a *receiver*. Often there a number of senders and many receivers. The sender transmits the message and is known as the *transmitter*.

Interpersonal communication

Watch two people having a conversation on the bus or in a cafe. They take it in turns to be sender and receiver. One will speak while the other listens. The second person will then make a reply before the first person speaks again. In such a conversation each person listens to what the other has to say before speaking. What they say depends on what was said before. There are times when one person may not quite hear what is said or may misunderstand it. This can lead to confusion. Comedy sketches on television often depend on this kind of misunderstanding.

A conversation is a form of communication between persons. We would describe it as *inter-personal*, (meaning between persons) communication. It can happen in many different ways. The sender and receiver do not have to be in the same place. They may have a conversation on the telephone. They do not even have to use speech. They may simply exchange letters. A conversation can take place using hand signing, morse code or a computer keyboard.

In any form of inter-personal communication the same pattern occurs. A message is transmitted by a sender to a receiver who works out what the message means. The receiver then becomes the sender and makes a reply. A conversation can continue in this way for as long as the two people want to go on talking.

Figure 12·1   Interpersonal communications

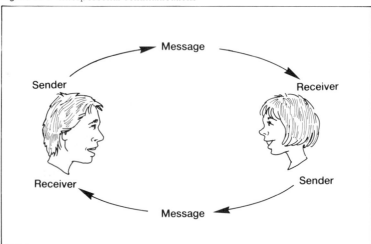

A conversation is an example of interpersonal communication.

Mass communication

Mass communication has many of the features of inter-personal communication. There are senders and receivers. Different media are used to transmit the messages. The people who receive those messages have to interpret the messages before they make sense.

There are also some important differences. Inter-personal communication involves a small number of people who share the roles of sender and receiver. In mass communication there is a small group of people who are the senders and a very large group who are receivers. The receivers have very little opportunity ever to become senders or to reply to the messages that they receive. This large group of receivers of mass communication are known as the *audience*.

Inter-personal communication can take place anywhere and at any time. People can gossip over the garden fence, on the bus, in the shops and while they are at work. It needs no special equipment and no organisation.

Mass communication is also everywhere around us. We hear the radio, read newspapers and magazines, see posters on hoardings, watch television and listen to records. We can easily forget that mass communication can only happen because someone made it happen and because there is the *technology* which makes it possible.

For mass communication to take place there must be some form of organisation and some kind of technology. Newspapers have to be published, television programmes, pop records and movies are produced, advertisements must be designed.

Inter-personal communication may also use technology. When you phone someone you depend on the electronic technology of the telephone. The technology for mass communication is different. It only permits messages to be sent one-way. There is no real way that you can answer back if you do not like what the person on the television is saying.

The organisation of the mass media which makes all of this possible can be vast. Producing a newspaper involves reporters and correspondents, editors and sub-editors, photographers and designers, typesetters and printers, distributors and newsagents.

Producing messages for mass communication is a form of *production* that is not very different from making motor-cars or baked beans. There are raw materials which are shaped into products which can then be sold. The finished product may be a newspaper or a television programme, a movie or a compact disc. The end result for the organisation which produces the mass communication is profit.

Discussion
It is often difficult to decide exactly what can be regarded as mass media. Which of these are examples of mass communication?

Figure 12.2

	Few producers, many receivers	Could not work without technology	No feedback	Is it mass media? Yes or no
A poster advertising cigarettes				
Gossip				
News at Ten on ITV				
A letter				
Two people talking on the telephone				
The *Daily Mirror*				
Writing on a wall				
Citizens Band radio				
A compact disc				
A small-ad in a personal column of the local paper				
A job application form				
A notice pinned to a notice-board				

12.2   The development of mass communication

Two thousand years ago scribes were employed to copy books by hand. They copied away in vast scriptoria to produce a regular supply of religious books and legal documents. They wrote on parchment made from animal skins. Although the work was slow the great number of scribes employed meant that fairly large numbers of books could be produced.

The books they produced were expensive. Few people could afford to buy them. Most went to abbeys and monasteries where they would be kept safely. The books contained ideas and knowledge which many believed should be kept from the ordinary people.

The problem which faced the medieval book publishers have been problems for the media industry ever since. They needed to find a way of producing books more cheaply. This meant doing away with copying by hand and introducing some form of technology. This was only worthwhile if they could produce more books. To make this worthwhile they needed a larger market.

The problem was partly solved by the invention of printing and by replacing parchment with paper. This made it possible to produce more books at less cost. A handful of printers could now do the work of thousands of scribes.

A sixteenth-century printing press.

Books and pamphlets are used to communicate information and ideas. This did not matter as long as they were only read by those who could be trusted with such knowledge. Political power was in the hands of the king and the church. Books were only acceptable if they supported their views.

Some means had to be found to control what went into the books and who could read them. This could be done by restricting the number of people who could print books. A printer would need a licence from the king or the bishop. *Censors* might be appointed to read printed material before it was published. Many books were printed in Latin, a language that few people understood. The state imposed taxes, called *stamp duties*, on printed books and newspapers to make them too expensive for the average person to buy. In this way only the rich, who could be trusted with the ideas, would obtain them.

These attempts to control the press were not always successful. In the seventeenth and eighteenth centuries a printing press could be set up quite easily. Anyone with a little capital could start their own newspaper. Most of the news was fairly local. News from London was two or three days old before it reached other parts of the country. News from Europe or America would be weeks old. Many of the newspapers and broadsheets were set up to attack the king or the government. It didn't matter that few people could read. The newspapers were read aloud in taverns and coffee houses.

Media technology

During the nineteenth century power-driven printing presses were introduced. The new machines could print faster and more cheaply but they were expensive to buy and to run. The newspaper publisher needed to sell even more newspapers to cover the cost of the new machines and make a profit. By this time the education system had improved and more people could read. The railways and the telegraph meant that news travelled faster.

Newspaper owners realised that as well as printing news they could also include advertisements. Manufacturers would pay to have their goods advertised and this helped to keep the price of the newspapers low. Low prices meant more readers. This was also good for the advertisers who reached a larger market. The modern newspaper began to develop.

Stamp duties had never been a good method of controlling the printing of news. They were only abolished when it became clear that they were no longer needed. The men who owned the new mass circulation newspapers were not likely to print things which offended those in power. The new 'press barons' had close personal links with the ruling classes. This was a far more powerful method of control than the Stamp Acts or newspaper censorship.

The twentieth century

Before the twentieth century the growth of mass communication had centred on the rise of the newspaper. The last eighty years have seen the development of many new forms of mass media. These have included the cinema, radio and television, recorded music and video.

Cinema replaced the old vaudeville theatres as a place to go for an evening out. Radio, television and recorded music brought mass communication into the home.

The new media industries still face the same problems. They still needed to produce for a large market at a low cost. As well as producing records, cassettes and videos the new media industries also need to manufacture the equipment on which they can be played. Control over the content of the media still causes concern. Films and videos have to be licensed before they can be shown publically. New laws were necessary to prevent excessive violence or pornography from reaching the nation's television screens.

In wartime working men gather round a pub radio to hear Sir Winston Churchill speak to the nation.

Discussion

The development of books and newspapers passed through three stages. At each stage the publishers used different methods of production, the media 'audience' or market changed and there were new problems of control.

Use the grid below to make a summary of the changes. How does the media industry in the twentieth century cope with the same problems?

Figure 12.3

	Method of production	The media audience	Means of control
The medieval scriptoria			
The printing press			
The press barons			

12.3   How the news is made

'This is the Nine O'Clock News.'

When you sit down in front of your television to watch the Nine O'Clock News you are seeing the end of a process of news production which began over twelve hours before. It is the result of days of careful planning and organisation involving hundreds of people.

Each 'newsday' begins with a meeting of the news editors whose job it is to put the news bulletins for the day together. They will look back over the way the news was presented on the previous day and then begin to plan the day ahead.

Producing a news bulletin on television needs careful organisation. Reporters have to write their stories. Camera crews have to be in the right place to get the best pictures. Interviews have to be arranged. Satellite link-ups have to be booked to bring reports and pictures from the other side of the world. If everyone sat around waiting for the news to happen there would be very little worth watching on the evening news.

A large part of each day's news can be predicted. Events like a royal wedding or the state opening of Parliament are known about months before they happen. People who are likely to be 'in the news' will have their days planned for them. The Prime Minister's diary is known well in advance. Many events happen at particular places at set times of day. The beginnings and ends of football matches, court appearances, conferences and demonstrations can be predicted fairly accurately. Those who want their activities reported will issue 'press releases' before the event. All of this makes it possible for news organisations to plan how they will cover the day's news.

Some news stories will 'break' unexpectedly. No one can predict an airline accident or a bank robbery. These stories will have to be covered as they happen. If a story 'breaks' in another part of the world it may be covered by correspondents. If there is no correspondent on the scene the story may have to come from another source. An important 'news source' is the *news agency*. The two largest are the Press Association and Reuters. They have reporters in every part of the world to collect stories which can be sold to newspapers and television. Foreign news may also be bought from other television news organisations, often using satellites to transmit it across the world.

Gatherers and processors

Throughout the day news stories, interviews, film and pictures will flow into the BBC news room.

Collecting the news is the job of the *news gatherers*. Many of these are specialists who only cover a particular type of story. There will be special correspondents for politics, crime, sport or a particular area of

the world. Other news gatherers deal with any area of news. These are the general reporters.

Once the news has been gathered it is handed over to the *news processors*. These are editors and sub-editors whose job it is to turn the news stories into the final news programme. News from agencies and other news sources is seen first by the 'copy taster' who throws most of it away. The 'copy taster' is an important *gatekeeper* who decides which items of news are 'newsworthy'.

One item in ten is passed on to the next line of sub-editors. Their job is to shape the news to make it fit into the time available. A midday news programme may last fifteen minutes. The evening news will last 25 minutes. It is here that the different pieces come together.

The news processor's job is to select the events, the words and the pictures which will make up the news bulletin. Even more of the news that has been so carefully collected during the day will be discarded. Some may be saved for another day and some may be passed on to other television news programmes such as 'Newsnight' and 'Panorama'.

The sub-editors are looking for material that has good 'news value'. It must be interesting for the viewer, up-to-date, and balanced. It must also be easy to understand. Material which is complicated will either be rejected or re-written to make it appear simple. An 'expert' may be brought in to explain things in a way everyone can understand. If the news for the day has been particularly gloomy the programme may end with a more cheerful story.

Even those stories which are to be used will be edited to make them fit the slot available. The script for the news reader will be written and re-written. Fifteen seconds of one film will be linked to 10 seconds of a map. An interview will be cut to 30 seconds. Even then there is the possibility that a late news item will cause the whole piece to be scrapped at the last moment.

As transmission time gets nearer the pressure increases. Most television news programmes are rehearsed to make sure that all of the pieces fit together smoothly. Even then changes may be made just as the programme is about to go on to the air.

Exactly at nine o'clock the captions will begin. A voice will announce 'This is the Nine O'Clock News read by ...'.

Projects

1. The television news rooms produce as many as three news bulletins each day. As the 'newsday' develops the news will change. Use a video-recorder to record the day's news from the BBC and from ITN. How does the news develop in each bulletin. In what ways are the BBC and ITN bulletins different?

2. Use the video of one news bulletin to study how a news programme is constructed. How much time is given to the news announcer and how much to filmed sequences? Who is interviewed on a particular news item, and who is not? How does the news bulletin achieve balance between different viewpoints?

3. Producing a television news bulletin is similar to producing a newspaper. Compare the ways in which different newspapers treat the same items of news.

12.4 Advertising

Advertising is all around us. It helps to pay for the newspapers and magazines we read and the television we watch. Advertising sponsorship promotes sport, helps charities and supports education. We see so many advertisements in a single day that we never have time to take them all in. Yet, they have an effect. Companies would not spend that amount of money if they were not getting something in return.

Each year over £2 000 000 000 is spent on advertising in Britain. Out of every £100 spent in the shops, nearly £2 goes towards the cost of advertising the products.

Producing advertisements

Advertising can be used to sell and to persuade. Anyone who has something to sell or a point of view to put across can advertise. Most people who want to advertise will go to an *agency*. Once the agency is clear about the client's requirements they will set about planning the *campaign*, designing the advertisements and buying the space in newspapers or on TV.

Figure 12·4 Spending on advertising, 1979

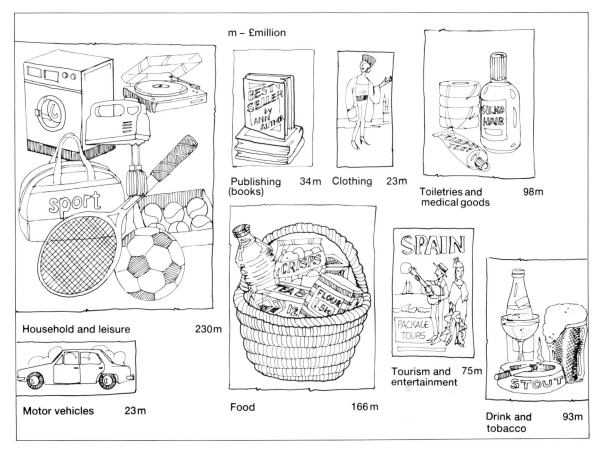

m – £million

Publishing (books) 34m   Clothing 23m   Toiletries and medical goods 98m

Household and leisure 230m

Motor vehicles 23m

Food 166m

Tourism and entertainment 75m

Drink and tobacco 93m

Dear Sir,
I'd like
to complain
about this
advertisement
because

Most advertisements are legal, decent, honest and truthful. A few are not, and, like you, we want them stopped.

If you would like to know more about how to make complaints, please send for our booklet: 'The Do's and Don'ts of Complaining'. It's free.

The Advertising Standards Authority. ✔

ASA Ltd., Dept. Z, Brook House, Torrington Place, London WC1E 7HN

The agency's aim will be to get the message across to the people the client wants to hear it. A wide choice of media can be used to place the 'ads'. Newspapers and magazines, poster sites, direct mail to potential customers, trade papers, radio and television could all be used. A large advertising campaign costing many millions of pounds will use any number of these to get the message across.

Advertisers are not free to say anything they wish. False or misleading statements are covered by the Trades Descriptions Act. Other laws cover advertising of cigarettes and alcohol. The Advertising Standards Authority checks that advertisements do not mislead the public.

Commercial break

Commercial television came to Britain in 1954. Before then there had only been one television channel run by the BBC and paid for by licence fees. The new commercial ITV channels were paid for by advertisements. *Franchises* were granted to a number of television companies to provide the programmes. Control over the new systems was in the hands of the Independent Broadcasting Authority, or IBA.

Although commercial television makes programmes it sells audiences. Months in advance the ITV companies publish their programme schedules. Each evening's viewing is carefully planned to produce a number of audiences. The early evening programmes are aimed at

Figure 12·5 Advertising by different media, 1979 (%)

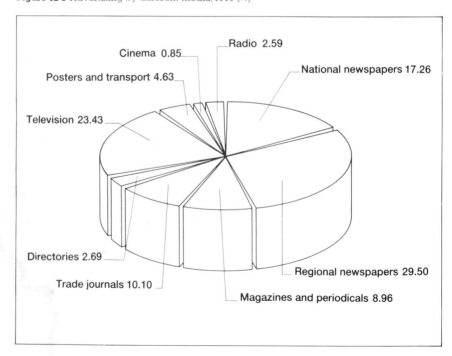

viewers who are coming in from work, getting a meal and sitting down to eat. The advertising will be aimed at busy mums and hungry families.

Later in the evening people will sit down to watch, often as a family group. The programmes and advertising will reflect this. When the youngest children have gone to bed the programmes will be different again. There will be more serious documentaries, crime dramas and thrillers. The main news programmes are usually later in the evening with programmes which attract smaller audiences even later.

At each stage of the evening the main advertisements will be aimed at the particular audience.

Knowing how the schedule is put together makes it possible for advertisers to plan their campaigns. In America whole programmes are sponsored by companies. Announcers will stop in the middle of a show to 'bring a message from the sponsor'. In Britain *spot advertisements* are used. These must be clearly separated from the programmes. Few adverts last longer than one minute, many are much shorter.

The advertiser pays for the time bought from the television company. It is important to get the message across quickly and effectively. When 'buying time' the advertiser must look for the size of the audience and its composition. The TV schedules and the audience research make it possible to aim a commercial at a specific audience. The cost of an advertising slot depends on the value of the audience to the advertiser.

It is also important to place the advertisement in the right context. The programmes that the viewers turn on to watch should create a good background to the advertisements. It would not make sense to advertise an airline in the middle of an air disaster movie or beer in a documentary on alcoholism.

Questions
1. What type of products do advertisers spend the most money on advertising?
2. More money is spent on advertising in regional newspapers than in the national papers. Why do you think this is?
3. Who would you go to if you wanted to conduct an advertising campaign?
4. Who controls how things can be advertised and what the advertiser can say about a product?
5. How does independent television 'sell audiences'?

12.5   Words and pictures

The first advertisments were made up only of words. There were no pictures. They were very similar to the modern small-ads and kept within the single columns of the newspaper. Editors would not allow advertisements to spread across more than one column or to use large type because they feared that it would distract the reader's attention from the news.

As the newspaper proprietors began to realise that advertising not only improved the look of the newspaper but also brought in more money, they began to change. The early printing methods made it very difficult to produce photographs in a newspaper. Advertisers had to make do with drawings to illustrate their products.

The advertising image

It is impossible today to think of advertising without thinking of pictures. Whether the advert is in a newspaper, a magazine or on television it is likely to involve a visual image. These images look real. They are meant to. They are, in fact, always manufactured in some way. Even when an advertisement uses a picture from real life it will have been cut down to make it fit the space and to direct attention to the important information.

Most advertising photographs are very carefully constructed to communicate a message. Words are used to add meaning to the pictures. The product that is being advertised is usually clearly shown either in a photograph or by its name. The message of the advert is communicated by the way in which the product is shown.

Many adverts include a picture of the *product* that they are trying to sell. The product is presented in some way in the advertisement. Often it is shown in its raw state and how it might be in use. An advertisement for paint may show the tin of paint and how it looks when it is on the walls.

When the product is shown it is often made into an example of a particular *type* of product. A very ordinary box of chocolates is made into an example of luxury or elegance. This can often be done by *associating* it with other items of that type. The chocolates will be photographed with expensive jewellery or fast cars which are used to *symbolise* extravagance.

Figure 12·6 The growth of advertising

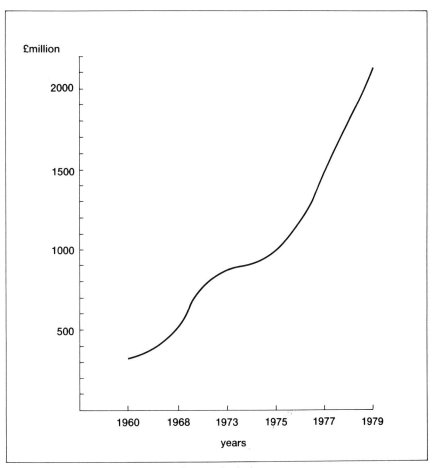

(All data from Dyer, G. Advertising as Communication)

Constructing the image

There are a number of components which go to make up any advertisement. As well as the product or its name, there is likely to be at least one person. Sometimes there are more. How that person looks is important. The clothes that are worn, the poses that have been taken, the expressions and actions are all carefully planned. If the photo includes a number of *people* the messages will be communicated in the way they relate to each other.

As well as people adverts also include *props.* These are objects which communicate a meaning that the advertiser wants you to link with the product. An expensive sports car in an advertisement for perfume is intended to make you link the perfume with speed and excitement. Props often have very little to do with the way the product is used in real life. Their job is to convey an impression.

People and props are shown in *settings.* The setting may be a darkened room or a mountain side, an ordinary kitchen or an expensive hotel. Whatever setting is shown, it is as important as both the people and the props. The setting also communicates messages about the product.

Putting people, props, settings and words together with a product in a particular way creates the advertisement. Nothing happens by accident. Every little detail has been planned to communicate exactly the message that the advertiser wants to convey.

Project: decoding advertisements

Advertisements can be examined to show how their messages are communicated. The way words and pictures are used and how the images are constructed can be analysed.

In this way advertisements can be decoded to show how they work. You can do this with advertisements from newspapers and magazines or videos of commercials from the television.

Having selected your advertisement you need to sort out the main items that are used to make it. What words are used? What do they tell you? Describe the pictures concentrating on what you can actually see.

You can now move on to meanings. What does the advert mean to you? Finally, write down the message that you think the advertiser is trying to get across. Use the grid oposite to help you.

Figure 12·6 Decoding advertisements

Will the '86 ketchup be even better than the '85?

Every August, the tomatoes in the Po Valley are ready for picking.

While they're still fresh they're bottled for Sainsbury's Italian Tomato Ketchup.

After one harvest, it's finito for another year.

Wine vinegar and spices add to the traditional flavour – but never tomato purée.

(Unlike most other ketchups there is nothing to mar the fresh natural taste.)

This isn't the easiest way to make a ketchup, but it is the best.

Which is why you'll find it at Sainsbury's.

Year in, year out. **Good food costs less at Sainsbury's.**

1. What is the product being advertised?	Sainsbury's Tomato Ketchup
2. What words are used on the advert? (if there is a great deal of text summarise the main points that are made) a. Headlines or large type b. Information about the product c. Other text	a. Will the '86 Ketchup be even better than the '85 b. fresh tomatoes, from Po Valley, added wine vinegar and spices, no puree. c. Good food costs less at Sainsbury's
3. Images? Photograph or artwork? a. Subject of illustration b. Setting c. Information about the product d. People How many? Doing what? Poses? Expressions? Clothes?	Ketchup bottles in a wine rack, dark background, lighting brings out label.
4. Choose any or more of the main parts of the advert What meanings do they convey to you? Why do you think they are included in the advertisement?	The headline and the photo are meant to show that the Ketchup is as good as vintage wine
5. What message do you think the advertiser is trying to get across? How successfully has the product been sold through the advertisement?	The advertiser is trying to make people associate the ketchup with wine and to make you think that it is something special.

12.6   Media effects

To the people of New Jersey in the eastern United States it was just another Hallowe'en. There was no television in 1938 but many people were listening to their radios. The evening's music was being played by Ramon Raquello from the Hotel Park Plaza in New York.

Suddenly the programme was interrupted by an urgent newsflash. Martian spaceships were in the sky over the United States and had landed near Grover's Mill. Alien beings had left the ships and were moving towards New York. The voice of the commander of the State Militia was heard telling people to keep calm. A radio amateur came on the air calling for help as the aliens attacked. Then the radio went quiet.

The result was panic. The roads were blocked with families trying to escape the advancing aliens. Phone lines were jammed as people tried to find out what was happening.

There was no Martian invasion. It was the first episode in the Orson Wells' production of 'The War of the Worlds'. The newsflash seemed so real that many people believed an invasion had taken place.

The active audience

A simple view of the way the media has an effect imagines that people sit in front of their television sets waiting to be told what to do and what to think. This view sees the audience as *passive*, like zombies waiting for their orders.

People are not like that. Mass communication may be 'one-way' but the 'receivers' do have some power over what is communicated. You can always turn the television off, or buy a different newspaper. The 'passive audience' view regards people as sponges, soaking-up whatever is put before them. You have only to think about how people watch television to see that this cannot happen.

Each person who reads a newspaper or watches television has to make sense of the messages that are received. Two people may interpret those same things quite differently. How you make sense of an advertiser's claims or a politician's statement depends on your past experience of the product, or of politics. Everyone has to act on the media messages in order to make sense of them. The media audience is not a passive audience. It is an *active* audience.

Response and reaction

The media's effects are seldom as spectacular as the effect of Orson Wells' radio play.

When an advertisement makes someone so interested in a product that they buy it the effect is short term. The person has made an individual *response* to the advertisement. The response is what the advertiser intended.

On another occasion the effect on the individual may be unintended. Television news pictures of violence or suffering are not intended to upset people but they sometimes do. The individual who is upset by such scenes is *reacting* to the scenes.

A collective reaction can take place when a large number of people react to something they see on television or read in the newspaper. Orson Wells' radio play led to a collective reaction. It was not something that was intended.

At other times the media intentionally try to make large numbers of people respond in a particular way. This collective response is often the result of a media campaign. The Live Aid concerts in 1985 were heard live by one-and-a-half-billion people across the world. The collective response raised millions of pounds for the world's starving people.

The producers of the media intend to produce a response in the audience, either individually or as a group. Sometimes the effect is an unintended reaction.

Bob Geldof at the Live Aid concert in aid of famine relief in Africa.

Discussion
Where would you put the following activities on the grid?
1. Copycat riots after watching scenes of violence on the television news.
2. Buying something that first caught your eye in a magazine advertisement.
3. Telephoning the television company to complain about a programme.
4. Joining with people who live nearby to start a Neighbourhood Watch scheme after you had all seen a Crimewatch programme on protecting your neighbourhood.

Figure 12.8

	Individual	Group
Response		
Reaction		

Long term effects

The effects of the media can be short term, over a period of hours or minutes, or long term, having an effect over many years. Many of the ways the media has an influence happen so slowly that it is difficult to realise that they are happening at all.

The media can have an influence on people's attitudes. Television documentaries and 'real-life drama' can cause people to change their views. In the 1960s 'Cathy Come Home', a television play about homelessness, had an important effect on attitudes towards the homeless.

As well as having an influence on how individuals see the world the media can have an effect on the wider society. The majority of the world's films and television programmes are made in America. The way-of-life they show is an American way-of-life. Programmes like 'Dallas', 'Miami Vice' and 'Dynasty' are set in a very different world from anywhere in Britain. Many people fear that the great amount of American television that is shown in Britain could have an effect on the British culture.

As well as changing attitudes the media can also confirm what people believe. The media tends to take a very traditional approach to different groups within society. In areas like the changing roles of women or black rights it tends to follow rather than lead public opinion. This may have the effect of slowing down changes which are long overdue.

12.7   Vocabulary

Audience   The receivers of mass communication messages.

Censorship   Controls over the stories and information that the media are allowed to publish.

Franchise   The licence granted to independent television and radio companies allowing them to broadcast.

Gatekeeper   An individual, usually an editor or sub-editor, who controls the flow of news and selects what is to be printed.

Inter-personal communication   Communication between two or more people.

Kissogram   A message, such as 'Happy Birthday', sent by a messenger in scanty clothing, to be delivered with a kiss.

Medium   The channel for communicating mass communication messages.

Message   Any communication. It can include items of news in a newspaper, information in an advertisement and the words in a pop song.

News agency   An organisation which employs its own correspondents to gather news which can be sold to newspapers and television.

Newsday   The day leading up to the publication of a news programme or newspaper.

Soap opera   A television serial based on domestic or family situations which is broadcast at least once a week over a period of time. The name originated from the early American television series that were sponsored by soap manufacturers.

Special correspondent   A journalist who specialises in a particular type of news or news from one part of the world.

Transmitter   An individual or an organisation who sends messages.

INDEX

ACKNOWLEDGEMENTS

We are grateful to the following for permission to reproduce photographs: Advertising Standards Authority, page 240; Anthro-photo, page 42 (photo: Irven Devore); BBC Enterprises, pages 237, 238; BBC Hulton, pages 32, 45, 127, 146, 156, 216, 217, 233, 235; Camera Press, pages 4, 8 above right (photo: Ray Green), 8 below left (photo: Tom Blau), 9 above left (photo: Lennox Smillie), 10 above (photo: Colin Davey), 27, 35 (photo: Peter Francis), 61, 73, 85 (photo: Wolfgang Roth/Bunte), 86 (photo: John Bulmer), 102, 140, 176, 181 (photo: Les Wilson), 126 (photo: Richard Owen), 164 (photo: Peter Abbey), 167 (photo: Srjda Djukanovic), 209 (photo: Benoit Gysembergh), 211 (photo: Andy Beard), 214 (photo: Mike Wells), 219, 222 (photo: Theo Noort), 110 (photo: Lionel Cherruault), 157 (photo: James Pickerell), J. Allan Cash, page 92; Ron Chapman, pages 8 below centre, 231; Coverdale & Fletcher, page 81; Fiat Auto UK, page 97; Sally and Richard Greenhill, pages 9 below, 41, 49, 55, 72 below left, 78, 89, 152, 159, 226; Susan Griggs Agency, page 139 (photo: Peter Boardman); The Guardian, pages 48, 83; John Hands, page 107; Sheelagh Latham, page 5 above; London Express News and Features, page 155 (photo: Dennis Caivus); London Features International, page 247; Lloyds Bank, page 135; The Daily Mail and the Mail on Sunday, page 190; Mothercare UK Ltd, page 44; Network, pages 5 below, 8 below right (photo: Barry Lewis), 39, 65, 72 below right (photo: Laurie Sparham), 98 (photo: Chris Davies), 179 (photo: Katalin Arkell), 185 below (photo: John Sturrock), 188 (photo: Steve Benbow); Oxfam, page 10 below; Photo Co-op, pages 14 (photo: Gina Glover), 121 (photo: Vicky White); Punch Publications, page 218; Rex Features, page 80; Sport and General Press Agency, page 29; Syndication International, page 153; United Nations, page 204; James C. Webb, page 36; Josiah Wedgwood & Sons Ltd, page 116.
Cover photograph by Longman Photographic Unit.